T0259945

Code Generation with Roslyn

Nick Harrison

Apress®

Code Generation with Roslyn

Nick Harrison
Lexington, South Carolina, USA

ISBN-13 (pbk): 978-1-4842-2210-2   ISBN-13 (electronic): 978-1-4842-2211-9
DOI 10.1007/978-1-4842-2211-9

Library of Congress Control Number: 2017934516

Managing Director: Welmoed Spahr
Editorial Director: Todd Green
Acquisitions Editor: Todd Green
Development Editor: Laura Berendson
Technical Reviewer: Matt Duffield
Coordinating Editor: Nancy Chen
Copy Editor: Kezia Endsley
Compositor: SPi Global
Indexer: SPi Global
Artist: SPi Global
Cover image designed by Freepik

Distributed to the book trade worldwide by Springer Science+Business Media New York, 233 Spring Street, 6th Floor, New York, NY 10013. Phone 1-800-SPRINGER, fax (201) 348-4505, e-mail orders-ny@springer-sbm.com, or visit www.springeronline.com. Apress Media, LLC is a California LLC and the sole member (owner) is Springer Science + Business Media Finance Inc (SSBM Finance Inc). SSBM Finance Inc is a **Delaware** corporation.

For information on translations, please e-mail rights@apress.com, or visit http://www.apress.com/rights-permissions.

Apress titles may be purchased in bulk for academic, corporate, or promotional use. eBook versions and licenses are also available for most titles. For more information, reference our Print and eBook Bulk Sales web page at http://www.apress.com/bulk-sales.

Any source code or other supplementary material referenced by the author in this book is available to readers on GitHub via the book's product page, located at www.apress.com/9781484222102. For more detailed information, please visit http://www.apress.com/source-code.

Printed on acid-free paper

This is dedicated to my loving wife Tracy.
We all have many dreams and aspirations,
but without the support and encouragement of a strong partner,
few of these dreams will be realized.
You often hear it said, "Behind every great man is a great woman".
In my case, it is "Standing beside a not so great man is a truly amazing woman".

Contents at a Glance

Contents

About the Author

 **Nick Harrison** is a software consultant living in Columbia, South Carolina. He has done full stack development on projects ranging from full featured Loan Origination Systems for prominent mortgage lenders to rapid prototypes for small startups. He has done full lifecycle development from initial inception through post deployment support.

Nick guided one mortgage company from initially doing 20M a month to 2B a month in funded volume.

Nick facilitated another mortgage company in understanding the code base for their loan origination system after they sued to get the source code from the vendor that was helping them with a strategy to resolve various problems identified with data access logic and other performance bottlenecks.

He has published articles and books on a wide range of technical topics including MVC, T4, Roslyn, software metrics, design patterns, and web design.

Contact him on Twitter: @Neh123us, where he also announces his blog posts, published articles, and speaking engagements.

About the Technical Reviewer

Matt Duffield is a senior software developer and author with experience in .NET and full stack development. He has over 18 years experience in software development. You can read his blog at `http://mattduffield.wordpress.com`.

Acknowledgments

Writing a book is a more involved task than you would think. It does not happen in a vacuum or by accident. It takes a lot of work from many people.

I would like to thank my family, who I know got tired of hearing the excuse, "sorry but I need to get some writing done".

I would like to thank the publishing team at Apress who no doubt stayed in a constant state of panic as so many deadlines went speeding by. Specifically, Laura Berendson and Nancy Chen were incredibly patient and supportive during this process.

Matt Duffield did a wonderful job keeping me honest and focused, making sure that I stayed on point and kept the examples and text clear and concise. He caught many problems that could be caught only by someone with his experience and expertise. I thank him for gently nudging me back in line with a patient reminder of "you might want to point out" or "I thank you meant".

Finally, I would like to thank former coworkers who lived through years of living with me working through some of these techniques. In this book, they are hopefully presented as a clean progressive push forward, but there was many false starts, much groping in the dark, and some frustration as not every bright idea worked as well in practice as it sounded in theory.

In the end, you, the readers, benefit from the hard work and patience of a wonderful team who helped see this work through to its completion. I hope you enjoy it and find something useful here.

CHAPTER 1

Introduction

The Problem with Business Logic

You have probably already figured this out, but business logic is hard. It is rarely logical, often doesn't follow discernable patterns, is riddled with exceptions, and changes often and quickly. This can be frustrating but it is the world we live in.

The business world is very competitive. These exceptions and apparent contradictions that drive us crazy often mean the difference between keeping a client and losing a client, between making a deal and losing the deal. Business environments often turn on a dime and when the environment changes, so must our applications. Having application that can change and respond at the speed of business is critical to survival in tough competitive markets.

This puts a lot of pressure on our business applications being able to adapt to change quickly. How do we respond to these challenges? In this book, we explore ways to make our applications more nimble so that they can change at the speed of business.

Develop/Test Deploy Takes Time

Every time we change code, we go through a similar cycle of develop, test, and deploy. These steps take time. Depending on how your application is structured and the processes and tools being used, this could take a lot of time. You can't deploy a single method or even a single class. The smallest unit of deployment is an individual assembly in the .NET ecosystem.

We can partition an application into separate assemblies to try to limit the scope and impact of such changes, but we need to balance runtime performance and time to market. If we split the logic across too few assemblies, we may be left needing to regression test the entire application for every change. Splitting the business logic across too many assemblies and we may have more metadata than runnable code in individual assemblies. Plus there comes a point where too many assemblies can slow down builds and even opening the solution.

▨ **Note** Performance concerns from the number of assemblies in an application are not likely to be an issue until you start dealing with hundreds or even thousands of assemblies. So putting each class in its own assembly is not an option.

© Nick Harrison 2017
N. Harrison, *Code Generation with Roslyn*, DOI 10.1007/978-1-4842-2211-9_1

We can also reduce the time we spend in the develop, test, and deploy cycle with Configuration Management tools. Tools such as continuous integration and automated unit tests can help streamline this cycle. Continuous integration tools allow the code in a repository to be integrated regularly, often with every check. automated unit testing allows you to define a collection of tests to be run against the output of the build with each integration. These tests can ensure with each integration that no new defects are introduced and that all requested features are implemented and are performing correctly. Because these integrations occur frequently, any problems that are introduced can be discovered quickly. The earlier a problem is discovered, the earlier it is to resolve.

It takes time to make code changes, test the changes, and deploy the changes. We can reduce this time by how we structure our solution. We can also add tools like continuous integration and automated testing to reduce this time, but no matter how much we optimize our processes or how we structure our solutions, we will never have software at the speed of business as long as we are stuck in this code/test/deploy loop.

Lookup Tables Are Easier to Modify, Verify, and Deploy

While we can't deploy a single method, we can deploy a single record from a lookup table. We can even deploy an update to a single column. To the extent that this allows us to influence business logic, this gives us lots of options to quickly make changes. The scope of the impact from the changes can be tightly controlled, verified, and easily deployed.

Modifying lookup tables can be as simple as a single SQL statement or as complex as a sophisticated interactive table maintenance screen. You can start simple and over time add sophisticated maintenance screens to push the maintenance from the control of developers to the hands of "power users". Verification can be as simple as running a report against the lookup tables to confirm that the correct data has been entered. Deployment can again be as simple as running SQL statements in the new environment or as complex as exporting key records from one environment and importing the same records in a new environment. This can easily be incorporated into your automated continuous integration strategy. Sophistication and complexity can grow as needed over time.

These configuration points must be designed and implemented in advance. We need to have the database structures in place to store the lookup data, and we also need code in place to reference and interpret the lookup data.

▨ **Note**   Chapter 2 focuses on various strategies for structuring this lookup data and how it might be interpreted.

We need to have code in place to reference and interpret this lookup data. This could take many forms.

- You may run a query to retrieve key configuration parameters.

- You may run a query to determine the next step in a complex workflow.

- You may run a query to evaluate which of key business rules are applicable.

- You may run a query that will actually implement and evaluate key business rules.

Lookup Tables Can Be Slow

In designing software, we often find that a good idea can easily morph into a bad idea. The potential problem with using lookup tables is that overusing or misusing lookup data can potentially slow your application down.

Structuring our applications so that every business decision is controlled by configuration values in lookup tables means that we can easily change any decision point on the fly, but it also means that we may have to make multiple-round scripts to the database to work out the logic for even a simple business transaction.

We need to be careful about how many decision points are configurable through lookup data and how much lookup data must be retrieved to complete a business transaction.

░ **Note**   You will see that in many cases, storing business logic in tables is much more efficient by leveraging the power of the database to filter and find the appropriate business rules. Just be wary of scenarios requiring multiple calls to the database.

We can have problems if we have to retrieve hundreds of records or make dozens of round trips to the database to complete a transaction. Consider the following business scenario:

- We cannot initiate a funding request after 3PM

- Unless it is a purchase, then the cutoff time is 4PM

- Unless the Group Manager has authorized an override

You may find similar business logic in a Mortgage Loan Origination System. You may see any number of changes to such business requirements over time. You can easily imagine individual states requiring different cutoff times. You might even see changes requested based on other properties such as Income Documentation Type or Property Type and so on. You may see changes requested to change who can authorize an extension and for how long. Even for a relatively straight forward business rule, the number of configuration points and options can grow quickly.

If you are not careful, you can introduce too many configuration points and sacrifice runtime performance in the name of configuration ease. The penalties for having a slow application can be worse than not being able to respond quickly enough to change.

Having Your Cake and Eating It Too

People don't like compromising. We want to have the best of both worlds. This is human nature. In a perfect world we would have the speed of compiled code and the maintenance ease that comes from table-driven logic. This book explores ways to reach this ideal state.

We explore how to structure lookup data to drive business in Chapter 2. We will see that there are a couple of patterns that we can follow for structuring lookup tables to drive business logic. We will look at some best practices to help guide when to use each approach and some tradeoffs that can be made to optimize some of these patterns to better fit your specific scenario.

Chapter 3 includes several case studies for taking common business logic tables and reviewing what the generated code to represent the encapsulated business logic might look like. We will not discuss how to generate code, only how the generated code would look. This should provide a template for pulling logic out of lookup tables regardless of the generation approach you take.

Chapter 4 introduces the Roslyn Compiler Services. We will explore how Roslyn can be used to build a type, a method, a conditional statement, a looping statement, etc. We will explore how to use Roslyn to generate code implementing the Business Logic described in our logic tables. Roslyn provides some nice options and simplifies some of the complexities and problems common with other code generation methods such as the CodeDom and T4.

Code generation often earns a bad reputation. If you are not careful, you can lose the ability to regenerate your code, which is key. To preserve this ability, we need to make sure that we don't ever directly change the code that we generate. Chapter 5 focuses on ways to preserve the integrity of generated code. We will talk about changing metadata or the generator instead of changing code. We will also talk about partial classes and inheritance to extend generated code. Here we will walk through some best practices for working in a living project that is based on generating code.

In Chapter 6, we discuss programmatically calling the compiler to compile the generated code. We will also explore best practices for deploying the newly generated assemblies. We will explore the complete lifecycle from a user, changing the logic data in a staging environment and verifying that the changes have the intended impact through deploying the new logic data along with the associated newly created assembly to the Production environment. We will also explore some best practices for minimizing the impact to Production when we make these deployments.

Reflection is the key to discovering and executing this generated code, to call the configured business logic. By definition, our generated code will not be known when the rest of the code was originally written. We will need to discover it to execute it. Chapter 7 walks through the mechanics of reflection to safely load a generated assembly, discover the types in the assembly, or create an instance of a specified type, and then call the relevant methods of the types that we find.

Finally in Chapter 8, we review all of the best practices we learned along the way.

What Is Not Covered

In this introduction, we touched on several related concepts that, while very important, are not addressed in this book. We only tangentially address the issues and best practices for separating business logic into separate assemblies. This is an important topic but not one that we will cover.

We will also skip over the issues with configuration management that we briefly mentioned earlier. Strong configuration management practices with continuous integration built on top of automated unit testing is very important, but discussing how to create this is outside the scope of this book. You can find great details for managing configuration management in *Beginning Application Lifecycle Management* (https://www.apress.com/us/book/9781430258124).

While this book will delve into creating the database structures needed to store and retrieve the data used to define and drive dynamic business logic, this is not a book on data modeling in general. We will provide some good advice and best practices, but this is far from a comprehensive guide to data modeling.

Summary

We live and work in chaotic world where business logic is guaranteed to change and change often. To stay relevant and competitive, our applications need to adapt and respond as quickly as possible. We have seen how it can be difficult to respond quickly with hard coded business logic. We have also seen how it is possible to respond to changes more quickly using table-driven business logic. While this solves the bottleneck inherent with the develop, test, deploy cycle, it can lead to runtime performance issues if the number of trips to the database to retrieve and build the business logic increases.

Throughout this book, we explore how to get the best of both worlds by using table-driven business logic to drive the generation of compiled code to implement business logic.

▓ **Note**   All code samples used throughout this book are written in C#. The SQL presented has been explicitly written and tested against SQL Server. Unless explicitly stated, the SQL should work with minimal changes against any ANSI-compliant database.

Next, we turn our attention to how to structure business logic in tables to supply the metadata needed for code generation.

CHAPTER 2

■ ■ ■

Putting Business Logic in Tables

A Catalog of Business Logic Tables

Broadly speaking, logic tables will fit into a couple of basic types. In this chapter, we identify four types of logic tables:

- Simple lookup table

- Input table with multiple parameters (decision table)

- Compound decision table

- Expression decision table

For each of these types, we will explore what they look like, discuss when they may be applicable, and step through some of the implementation details for proper implementations.

Simple Lookup Table

Lookup tables are often overlooked as a repository for business logic. Often they are viewed as nothing more than a simple location for pulling the values for a drop-down list. In many cases, they are given so little respect that the design falls into the trap of the "One True Lookup Table"—OTLT.

OTLT is an anti-pattern of database design. The basic justification for them goes something like this:

- I have all these lookup values

- Each lookup list is rather small

- We are likely to have lots of different lookup types

- I don't want to have to change the data model every time I add a new lookup type

- Rather than pollute the data model with lots of little tables, let's put all of these lookup values in one table

On the surface, this seems perfectly reasonable and sounds like it should lower the total cost of maintenance since you don't have to create a new table every time you add a new lookup type. We are, after all, always looking for ways to streamline maintenance. However, there are hidden costs to data quality.

In its simplest form, the OTLT might look like Figure 2-1.

© Nick Harrison 2017
N. Harrison, *Code Generation with Roslyn*, DOI 10.1007/978-1-4842-2211-9_2

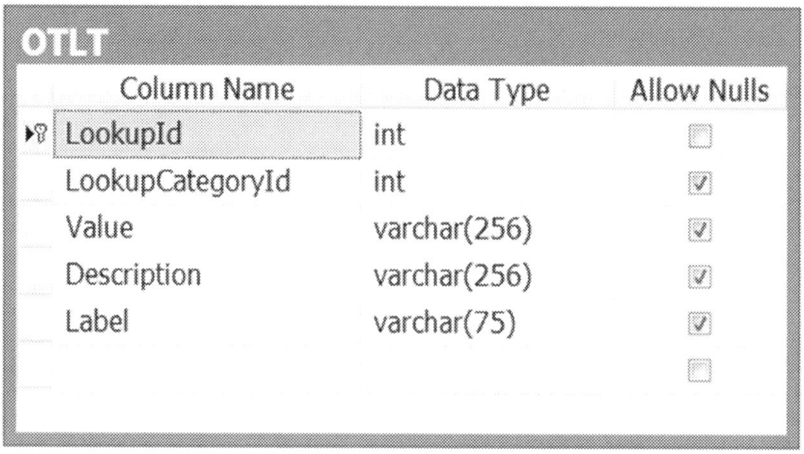

OTLT		
Column Name	Data Type	Allow Nulls
▸⬚ LookupId	int	☐
LookupCategoryId	int	☑
Value	varchar(256)	☑
Description	varchar(256)	☑
Label	varchar(75)	☑
		☐

Figure 2-1. *The basic structure of the One True Lookup Table*

There are a couple of problems with this design.

▪ **Tip**   We often have a vested interested in keeping logic tables separate from entity tables. This way we can potentially use the logic tables in multiple lines of business applications as needed, but we don't want to keep lookup tables separate from the entity tables.

Lookup tables need to be incorporated into your data model. You'll want to incorporate them in a big way. By keeping each lookup category defined in a separate table, we can easily define all of the constraints implied by the lookup values. This will do wonders for data integrity, but would be very difficult in an OTLT.

▪ **Note**   You can get the same data integrity constraints with an OTLT but few even attempt it. The check constraints would be massive and would have to be updated every time a new lookup type was stored. There goes your lower maintenance costs!

Without proper constraints, there is nothing to prevent someone from specifying that the state is "North East" or that the occupancy for a mortgage is "Full Doc". The constraints will have to be enforced somewhere or you will always have dirty data.

Another problem is the size of the columns. Because you don't know what type of values will be stored ahead of time and you have to explicitly design them to store anything, the Value column is loosely typed and all of the fields are much bigger than they need to be. Some implementations may even resort to NVARCHAR(MAX) for the value or description. The flexibility designed into this solution means that you cannot put a reasonable maximum size for these fields. With such large sizes for these pivotal fields, you will eventually contain dirty data unless you add even more complexity to the already complex constraint checks on this table.

> ■ **Note** The check constraint will be a giant `case` statement with a separate clause for every `LookupCategoryId`. Maintaining the complex constraint checks will eventually fall to the wayside, as it will eventually be viewed as more trouble than it is worth.

Let's consider a classic role for a lookup table. We know that in various places we will prompt for the state in an address. We don't want the users to be able to type the state in directly. We want to force the users to select from a list of valid state options. Our first pass at a lookup table may look like Figure 2-2.

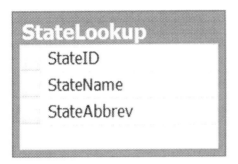

Figure 2-2. *Example of a lookup table specifying the state name and abbreviation for the valid states*

> ■ **Caution** Like all guiding principles, there are exceptions. By the end of this chapter, we will revisit the OTLT with a practical application.

We would use the lookup table in our data model, as shown in Figure 2-3.

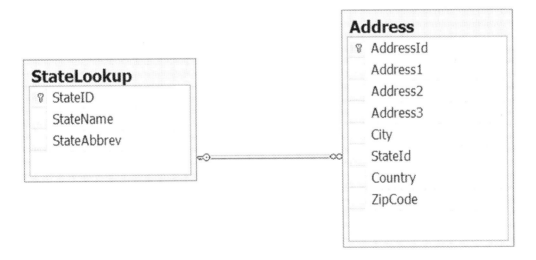

Figure 2-3. *Using the lookup table with transaction data*

With this data model, we can easily define the constraints to limit states to only the states that have been defined. In fact, we get those constraints without any work on our part beyond simply defining the foreign key relationship. This means that we will never have to worry about dirty data in this field.

So far so good, but this doesn't really have any business logic (beyond keeping track of which states you do business in). However, if you look through your source code, you might find business logic like that shown in Listing 2-1.

Listing 2-1. Repeated switch Statements Often Represent a Design Problem

```
switch (state)
{
    case "AL":
        // Sales Tax for Alabama
        break;
    case "FL":
        // Sales Tax for Florida
        break;
    case "GA":
        // Sales Tax for Georgia
        break;
    case "KY":
        // Sales Tax for Kentucky
        break;
    case "NC":
        // Sales Tax for North Carolina
        break;
}
```

▓ **Caution**   This could grow to a large `switch` statement if you do business in all 50 states, not to mention painful to maintain as you grow and do business in new states and have to find and update all of these `switch` statements.

A common best practice for eliminating `switch` statements like this is to replace them with an object hierarchy (Figure 2-4) and let polymorphism work through the differences. Here you might have an object for each state and expose a property for the sales tax. Combine this with a factory to return the correct object and simply reference the `SalesTax` property. This object hierarchy is represented in Figure 2-4.

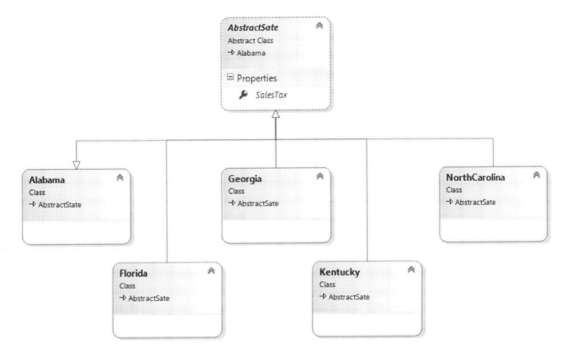

Figure 2-4. *Sample object hierarchy to replace the case statement*

Another option is to incorporate this logic into the lookup table. You can easily extend the data model to include sales tax (Figure 2-5).

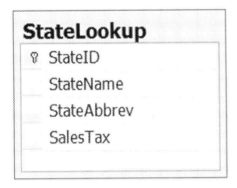

Figure 2-5. *Extending the lookup table to include limited business logic*

Now you can replace the business logic in the `switch` statement by simply retrieving the `SalesTax` value from the corresponding record in the lookup table. Next, you will see how this simple lookup table can become one of the inputs into a lookup table with multiple input parameters to handle more complex business logic.

▓ **Note**   This is not meant to disparage the approach with the object hierarchy. This is often still needed, but the evaluation of key fields like `SalesTax` can be initialized in the base class using such a lookup table

---

Lookup Tables with Multiple Input Parameters (Decision Tables)

There are many types of lookup tables. You just saw a lookup table in its simplest form. For simple cases of populating a drop-down list and associating simple business rules with the selected value, this is all you would need, but you'll often have more complex scenarios.

You may even find that a single lookup value points to many potential values and you need additional input parameters to pick the correct one. Hence, the decision table. Consider some of these scenarios:

- State specific late payment penalties that vary by state, lien position, etc.

- Shipping charges vary based on a range of weight and distance.

- Interactive questionnaires where the answer to one question determines the next question to ask.

You could express the business logic for each of these scenarios in code, but the code would be difficult to maintain and difficult to verify, leaving our application not very adaptive. Instead, it is much better to store the criteria in lookup tables that can easily be updated and verified. Let's look at how you could structure lookup tables to represent these business scenarios.

State-Specific Business Logic

If your application handles business in multiple states, you will eventually encounter state-specific business logic. It can be a nuisance. For any given business rule, chances are each state will have subtle variation on it. Often these business rules will be more complex than the simple example of determining the sales tax that you just saw.

Considering the scenario of state-specific rules for applying a late penalty to a mortgage payment. You first need to consider the loan level characteristics that are used to evaluate late payment penalties. You also need to consider the meaning of the penalty once it is deemed to be applicable. For each rule, note that the actual penalty can be composed of the following components:

- Minimum amount that can be charged

- Maximum amount that can be charged

- Percentage of payment that can be charged

Most states will have part of these components for a late penalty. Some may have all of these components. The penalty will often be worded as follows:

The penalty for a late payment shall be 5% of the monthly payment, not to exceed $150, and in all cases will be at least $25.

You next need to survey the various loan-level attributes that can be used to determine which late payment penalty will apply. For these purposes, let's assume that we have determined that the following loan-level attributes are used:

- Lien position

- Occupancy

- Property type

- Number of days late

Not all states will be concerned with every field, but we have determined that these four fields will be enough to determine applicability for a late payment penalty. Given this information, you can define a late payment penalty business rule with the lookup table shown in Figure 2-6.

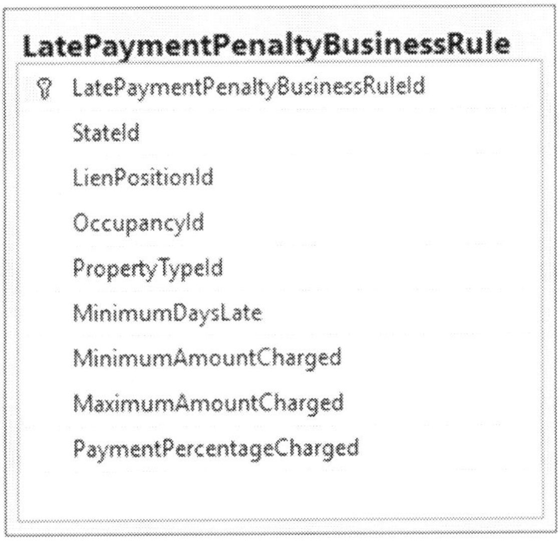

Figure 2-6. *Business rule logic for the late payment penalty business rules*

The StateId column will be a foreign key back to the StateLookup table that you saw in the previous section. The various other ID columns will be foreign keys to similarly defined tables. The MinimumDaysLate column will define how late the payment needs to be before the penalty can be applied. The various Charged columns will collectively define the penalty that will be applied.

▓ **Note**   Input parameters on a decision table will often be foreign keys to simple lookup tables or specify a range of continuous data.

The first five columns collectively define the criteria for applying the penalty. The final three columns define what the penalty will be. To determine which penalty to apply, you can run the query shown in Listing 2-2.

Listing 2-2. Sample Query for Evaluating Prepayment Penalty Rules

```
DECLARE @StateId INT;
DECLARE @LienPositionId INT;
DECLARE @OccupancyId INT;
DECLARE @PropertyTypeId INT;
Declare @DaysLate int;
```

```
SELECT  [MinimumAmountCharged], [MaximumAmountCharged], [PaymentPercentageCharged]
FROM    [dbo].[LatePaymentPenaltyBusinessRule]
WHERE   Stateid = @StateId
        AND ( Lienpositionid = @LienPositionId
                OR Lienpositionid IS NULL )
        AND ( OccupancyId = @OccupancyId
                OR OccupancyId IS NULL )
        AND ( PropertyTypeId = @PropertyTypeId
                OR PropertyTypeId IS NULL )
        AND MinimumDaysLate <= @DaysLate
```

This query accepts all of the loan-level attributes we identified as defining the business rule. The query returns the details for the actual penalty identified as being applicable. Earlier we stated that each state may not necessarily include all of the attributes in their definition for the late penalty. We accommodate this by allowing the columns to be null, which will be interpreted as "I don't care". So if a state does not care about the property type, the values for the PropertyTypeId column will be null and will not filter the results.

▓ **Tip**   For this example, there should only be one row returned. In some cases, you may have multiple rows and it may be the responsibility of the user to select an option from the returned results. In such cases, you may want to add a Priority column and sort the results based on this column. That way, the result that you would prefer the user select will be the first one returned.

With this query, we can easily determine whether or not a late payment penalty is applicable and retrieve the components needed to apply the penalty. The definition and rules for when it applies are encapsulated in the lookup table so the code you write does not have to change as the business rules change, unless a new rule adds a new loan-level attribute to consider. By the end of this chapter, you will see how to overcome even this restriction because your input parameters change frequently.

Shipping Charges

Any e-commerce site will have to deal with shipping charges. Often there may be a great many dynamic properties going into this calculation, and the key values will change over time to take advantage of market changes or to create promotions and drive business.

Let's consider a simple scenario where we determine the shipping charges based on the weight of what is being shipped and the distance that it needs to ship. To add an extra twist, we also need to base the logic off of time constraints, or rather date constraints. So the rates that apply could change from day to day. We need to remember what the rates were when the order was placed so that we can apply the advertised rate when the product ships, just in case the OrderDate and ShipDate are not the same.

▓ **Tip**   Business rules are often date- or time-specific, so marking such business rules with effective and expiration dates makes it easier to rerun transactions based on outdated business rules to honor a previous commitment or to deploy rules before they are accepted.

In this simple example, you can have any number of "pricing tiers" based on the distance being shipped and when the order was placed. Each tier will have an associated PricePerOunce for the weight of the item being shipped. You can define these rules in the table shown in Figure 2-7.

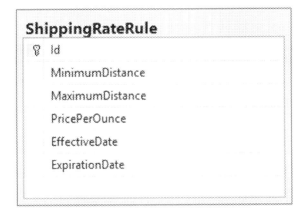

Figure 2-7. Business rule logic for the shipping rate business rules

The minimum and maximum distance columns will define the tiers. You also need to compare the order date to the effective and expiration dates to verify that we have the correct PricePerOunce that was in effect when the item was ordered. You need to allow the tiers to be open ended, so in some cases, you may not have a value for minimum or maximum distance. Ideally at least one should be set to properly define a tier, and if both are entered, you should expect the minimum to always be less than the maximum.

░ **Tip**   The business rules for the distance columns can be defined as constraints on the table, as an added layer of protection to ensure that they are adhered to.

You also have assumptions that there should not be overlaps or gaps in the tiers or in the date ranges defined by the Effective and Expiration Date columns. These requirements are harder to implement with constraints on the table and should be confirmed during the validation phase.

░ **Caution**   If there are gaps in either the pricing tiers or the effective date ranges, you could wind up with no shipping charges being associated with an order, which might be good for business but bad for profit. This will need to be covered during validation using reports against the lookup table.

To determine the shipping charges, query this table, passing in ShippingDistance and OrderDate. The query will return the PricePerOunce and you then leave it to the calling program to calculate the cost of shipping the items that were ordered (see Listing 2-3).

Listing 2-3. Simple Query for Evaluating the Sample Shipping Rules

```
DECLARE @DistanceToShip INT;
DECLARE @ShipDate DATETIME;

SELECT [PricePerOunce]
FROM   [dbo].[ShippingRateRule]
WHERE  ( @DistanceToShip >= [MinimumDistance]
         OR  [MinimumDistance] IS NULL )
       AND ( @DistanceToShip <= [MaximumDistance]
```

```
              OR  [MaximumDistance] IS NULL )
    AND ( @ShipDate >= [EffectiveDate]
              OR [EffectiveDate] IS NULL )
    AND ( @ShipDate <= [ExpirationDate]
              OR [ExpirationDate] IS NULL )
```

Usually the lowest tier will not have minimum distance defined and the top tier will not have a maximum distance defined, so both tiers will be open ended. It is also common for the rates that are currently in effect to have an EffectiveDate set but not have an ExpirationDate defined until a new set of rates is ready to be made active.

▨ **Note**   Anticipate much more complex rules in a real system. You will revisit this scenario shortly and learn about better ways to handle this complexity.

Interactive Questionnaire

Many applications need an interactive questionnaire where the questions are dynamically determined. Potentially the answer to one question may determine the next question. This may be useful for an online employment application, a satisfaction survey, a context sensitive help system, or a personalized squeegee page.

The more restrictions you can place on the types of answers that could be given, the easier this will be. In the simplest form, you would restrict this to simple yes/no questions. The table structures would look like Figure 2-8.

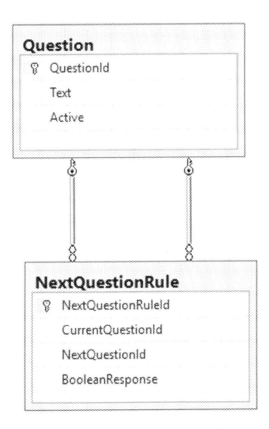

Figure 2-8. *Interactive question data model*

With this data model, you can support multiple questions associated with either response. Both responses could potentially trigger the same question, each response could trigger a different set of questions, or a response might halt new questions by leaving the NextQuestionId blank.

If you need to support multiple types of responses, simply replace the BooleanResponse column with one or more lookup table foreign keys depending on the types of answers you support. You can also use a pair min/max columns if the answers don't fit into a discrete value from an associated lookup table. The interpretation for this type of business logic will be handled in application code as the user answers each question.

Compound Decision Table

In the decision tables we have looked at so far, each record has uniquely defined a rule. This will not always be the case. The rules so far have been defined by joining the various attributes specified with and operators, but sometimes you may need to specify more than one value for specific attributes in the rule definition. For example, going back to the shipping costs example that you saw earlier, you may want to be able to define a special shipping plan based on multiple products.

To accommodate this structure, we will make a couple of changes to the original decision table. Let's start by separating the action from the definition for the rule. We will also add a couple of new product attributes to make the rules more interesting and realistic; see Figure 2-9.

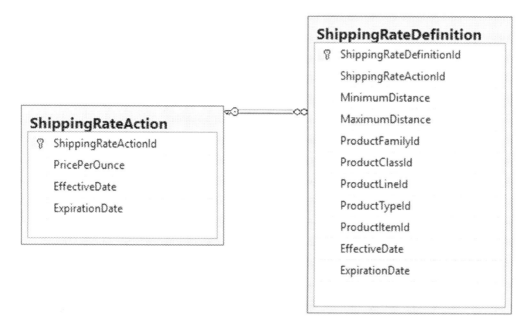

Figure 2-9. *A compound decision table for shipping rules*

Notice that we have a one-to-many relationship between the Action (ShippingRateAction) and the Definition (ShippingRateDefinition) tables. With this layout, the action will apply as long as any of the associated Definition records evaluate to true. We evaluate the rule by identifying the actions that have at least one associated Rule Definition record evaluate to true. We don't care how many Rule Definition records evaluate to true. As long as one evaluates to true, the action is applicable. In many cases, a single order may have multiple valid results. This is not a problem. You can add a priority column and sort by that column to select the preferred action. The query to make this work is similar to the original query with just a couple of tweaks (see Listing 2-4).

Listing 2-4. Simple Query for Evaluating a Compound Decision Table

```
DECLARE @DistanceToShip INT;
DECLARE @ShipDate DATETIME;
DECLARE @ProductFamilyId INT;
DECLARE @ProductClassId INT;
DECLARE @ProductLineId INT;
```

```
DECLARE @ProductTypeId INT;
DECLARE @ProductItemId INT;

SELECT  [PricePerOunce]
FROM    dbo.ShippingRateAction
WHERE   ( @ShipDate >= [EffectiveDate]
          OR [EffectiveDate] IS NULL )
        AND ( @ShipDate <= [ExpirationDate]
              OR [ExpirationDate] IS NULL )
        AND ShippingRateActionId IN (
        SELECT  ShippingRateActionId
        FROM    dbo.ShippingRateDefinition
        WHERE   ( @DistanceToShip >= [MinimumDistance]
                  OR [MinimumDistance] IS NULL )
                AND ( @DistanceToShip <= [MaximumDistance]
                      OR [MaximumDistance] IS NULL )
                AND ( @ShipDate >= [EffectiveDate]
                      OR [EffectiveDate] IS NULL )
                AND ( @ShipDate <= [ExpirationDate]
                      OR [ExpirationDate] IS NULL )
                AND ( @ProductFamilyId = [ProductFamilyId]
                      OR ProductFamilyId IS NULL )
                AND ( @ProductClassId = [ProductClassId]
                      OR ProductClassId IS NULL )
                AND ( @ProductLineId = [ProductLineId]
                      OR ProductLineId IS NULL )
                AND ( @ProductTypeId = [ProductTypeId]
                      OR ProductTypeId IS NULL )
                AND ( @ProductItemId = [ProductItemId]
                      OR ProductItemId IS NULL ) );
```

Expression Decision Table

The various decision tables that you have looked at so far give you a great deal of flexibility for structuring business logic in the tables, but they do have a weak point. It is not always possible to know every possible attribute that could be used for designing a business rule up front. Over time, the ongoing maintenance of adding new fields as they are needed add up and can be problematic.

You need a way to keep all the flexibility you want without incurring extra maintenance costs, but to do this, you need to explicitly violate a guiding best practice that you learned about at the beginning of this chapter. You will also adopt another anti-pattern called Entity Attribute Value (EAV). Generally though, you need to be avoid adopting anti-patterns and best practices are best practices for a reason!

You will incorporate the One True Lookup Table (OTLT) and the Entity Attribute Value (EAV) anti-pattern. Both of these are anti-patterns for similar reasons. They are popular because they allow you to extend the data model without having to make database structure changes. They are also problematic for similar reasons. Because these table structures are generalized to handle multiple scenarios, they are open to data integrity issues.

▓ **Tip** You can mitigate these risks to a certain extent by isolating these data models from the transaction system. Ideally keep these tables in a separate schema from the transaction system. Also maintaining this data should be the purview of a rules designer and not a casual application user.

Similar to the compound decision table, expression decision tables are split across two tables. We will have an Action table and a Detail table. These are conceptual names for these tables. In any practical implementation, they may take on more specific meaningful names. Unlike with compound decision tables, every associated detail must be passed.

Expression lookup tables are not evaluated in the database. They are always in code. We will explore their evaluation in detail in the next chapter.

Summary

You learned a lot of material here. You saw examples of storing business logic in several different types of tables from simple lookup tables to decision tables and compound decision tables and even expression decision tables.

For simple business rules, the simple lookup table may be all you need. If you have more complex rules that can be expressed with a well-known and static set of attributes then the standard decision table or perhaps a compound decision table may be your best option. When the set of potential attributes is likely to change or is already relatively large, consider using an expression decision table.

CHAPTER 3

Pulling Table Driven Logic Into Code

Overview

In Chapter 2, we explored various approaches for storing business logic in tables. You can structure your business logic in a variation or combination of the tables discussed. You have a lot of flexibility here. You just need to understand the business that you are working in and have some creativity.

Now you will turn your attention to what the logic stored in these tables would look like expressed in code.

Note   Not all of the examples you looked at so far are necessarily good candidates for structuring in code. These are advanced techniques that are not necessary in all cases. Follow the simplest approach that solves the problem.

- If the logic can readily be interpreted through a query, keep it in the database.

- If implementing the logic requires filtering through a large number of records to find the applicable rules, let the database handle the filtering. Databases are designed to churn through such filtering exercises.

- If it would require multiple round trips to the database to implement the logic for a common transaction, it may be a good candidate for bringing over to code.

- If the logic is interactive where the selection of the next rule depends on the outcome of a previous rule, this logic should be moved to code.

Here we will explore some examples that lend themselves nicely to being structured in code. One common pattern you will see is to filter the applicable rules in the database and then evaluate the selected rules or associated actions in code. Use the combination that suits your requirements the best.

Treating Lookup Tables as Enums

Even if you have no more business logic in your tables than simply storing a list of valid values, you can easily pull this into code and reap some benefits. Every application will have lots of lookup values. Even if you follow the One True Lookup Table anti-pattern, you can still benefit from structuring the lookup types as enums in your code. Consider a system with the following lookup types:

- LoanPurpose (see Table 3-1)
- Occupancy (see Table 3-2)
- PropertyType (see Table 3-3)

Lookup Data

Table 3-1. *Sample Lookup Data for LoanPurpose*

Loan Purpose ID	Name	Short Description
1	BusinessLaunching	Launch a new business
2	HomePurchase	Buy a home
3	HomeImprovement	Make home improvements
4	Investment	Finance investments
5	DebtConsolidation	Cash out to pay off debts
6	Education	Finance education
7	EmergencyExpendenture	Emergency funds to handle an unforeseen expense
8	CarPurchase	Buy a car
9	Wedding	Finance a wedding
10	Travel	Finance travel plans

Table 3-2. *Sample Lookup Data for Occupancy*

Occupancy ID	Name	Short Description	Long Description
1	OwnerOccupied	Owner Occupied	Property is occupied by the owner
2	SecondHome	Second Home	Property is a part-time residence for the owner
3	InvestmentProperty	Investment Property	Property is used as an investment and is never the owner's residence

Table 3-3. *Sample Lookup Data for PropertyType*

PropertyTypeId	Name	Short Description
1	DetachedHouse	Detached single family residence
2	SemiDetachedHouse	Semi-detached houses with front, rear, and any one side or both sides open
3	Townhome	An attached dwelling that is not a condo
4	Condominium	Single, individually-owned housing unit in a multi-unit building
5	BrownStone	Multi-floor row house with a brown sandstone facade

Code

▓ **Tip**   Code written using the following enums will be easier to write, understand, and maintain.

Given this lookup data, you could easily create enums as shown in Listing 3-1.

Listing 3-1. Sample Code Generated from the Metadata in the Lookup Tables

```
public enum LoanPurpose
{
    [Description("Launch a new business")]
    Business Launching = 1,
    [Description("Buy a home")]
    HomePurchase = 2,
    [Description("Make home improvements")]
    HomeImprovement = 3,
    [Description("Finance investments")]
    Investment = 4,
    [Description("Cash out to pay off debts")]
    DebtConsolidation = 5,
    [Description("Finance education")]
    Education = 6,
    [Description("Emergency funds to handle an unforeseen expense")]
    EmergencyExpendenture = 7,
    [Description("Buy a car")]
    CarPurchase = 8,
    [Description("Finance a wedding")]
    Wedding = 9,
    [Description("Finance travel plans")]
    Travel = 10
}

public enum Occupancy
{
    [Description("Owner Occupied")]
    OwnerOccupied = 1,
    [Description("Second Home")]
    SecondHome = 2,
    [Description("Investment Property")]
    InvestmentProperty = 3
}

public enum PropertyTypes
{
    [Description("Detached single family residence")]
    DetachedHouse = 1,
    [Description("Semi-detached houses with front, rear and any one side or both sides
    open")]
    SemiDetachedHouse = 2,
    [Description("An attached dwelling that is not a condo")]
```

```
    Townhome = 3,
    [Description("Single, individually-owned housing unit in a multi-unit building")]
    Condominium = 4,
    [Description("Multi floor row house with a brown sandstone facade")]
    BrownStone = 5
}
```

▨ **Note**   You may need to do a little finessing with the project structure to have these generated components isolated to a single assembly that can be regenerated and redeployed on demand. We will explore these deployment concerns in Chapter 7.

▨ **Tip**   It is always a good idea to include as comments or extended attributes in your generated any comments available in the metadata.

Table-Driven Hello World

A Hello World example is not exactly as contrived as it may initially seem. Imagine a content management system with a decision table to support determining the appropriate greeting for a user (see Figure 3-1).

For this CMS system, you may want to define rules controlling the greeting. Say you want to customize the greeting based on the time of day, gender, and marital status of the user. You could have a decision table like the one shown in Figure 3-1.

Figure 3-1. *Sample data model for greeting rules*

Data

Load the decision table with the records shown in Table 3-4, which will define a dozen rules for greeting men differently from married women and single women. We also get several bands for adjusting the greeting based on the time of day.

Table 3-4. *Sample Data for Greeting Rules*

Greeting Rule ID	HourMin	HourMax	Gender	MaritalStatus	Greeting
1	NULL	11	1	NULL	Good Morning Mr.
2	NULL	11	2	1	Good Morning Mrs.
3	NULL	11	2	2	Good Morning Ms.
4	12	17	1	NULL	Good Afternoon Mr.
5	12	17	2	1	Good Afternoon Mrs.
6	12	17	2	2	Good Afternoon Ms.
7	18	22	1	NULL	Good Evening Mr.
8	18	22	2	1	Good Evening Mrs.
9	18	22	2	2	Good Evening Ms.
10	23	NULL	1	NULL	Good Night Mr.
11	23	NULL	2	1	Good Night Mrs.
12	23	NULL	2	2	Good Night Mrs.

▨ **Note** Over time you may discovered that greeting women differently based on marital status is antiquated and wish to drop this designation. Such a change is easily accommodated by changing the lookup data without changing any of the code that evaluates the data in the lookup data. You chose to set the MaritalStatus to null for all records and then simply delete the records that are no longer needed when the Gender = 2. Alternately, you could update the Greetings when Gender = 2 to be the same for both values in the MaritalStatus column. You have many options, none of which will require that you actually have to change code.

Code

You can implement the business logic implied by this decision table with code like Listing 3-2.

Listing 3-2. Code Generated to Implement the Greeting Rules Defined in Table 3-4

```
public class GreetingRules
    {
        public string Rule1(IGreetingProfile data)
        {
            if (data.Hour > 11) return null;
            if (data.Gender != 1) return null;
            return "Good Morning Mr. " + data.LastName;
        }

        public string Rule2(IGreetingProfile data)
        {
            if (data.Hour > 11) return null;
            if (data.Gender != 2) return null;
            if (data.MaritalStatus != 1) return null;
            return "Good Morning Mrs. " + data.LastName;
        }
```

```
    public string Rule3(IGreetingProfile data)
    {
        if (data.Hour > 11) return null;
        if (data.Gender != 2) return null;
        if (data.MaritalStatus != 2) return null;
        return "Good Morning Ms. " + data.LastName;
    }

    public string Rule4(IGreetingProfile data)
    {
        if (data.Hour < 12) return null;
        if (data.Hour < 17) return null;
        if (data.Gender != 1) return null;
        return "Good Afternoon Mr. " + data.LastName;
    }
}
```

A couple of key points to consider:

- You will need an interface providing a property for each parameter in the decision table.

- If the rule passed, the return value should be populated with the details from the rule action.

- If the rule did not pass then the return value will be null or empty.

- In the GreetingRules class, you define a method for each rule, and each method should have the same signature, making it easier to discover the rules at runtime.

- Based on your business logic and specific needs, you may need to run all rules and review the ones that passed, or you may be satisfied knowing that any rule passed and can stop evaluating rules as soon as you see one that passes. In this case, we expect to have only a single rule pass, so we could stop evaluation as soon as we find a rule that passes.

For this example, the IGreetingProfile can be as simple as Listing 3-3.

Listing 3-3. Definition of the IGreetingProfile Interface Used by the Generated Greeting Rules

```
public interface IGreetingProfile
{
    int Hour { get; set; }
    int Gender { get; set; }
    int MaritalStatus { get; set; }
    string FirstName { get; set; }
    string LastName { get; set; }
}
```

When you are ready to evaluate these rules, you will define an object that implements this interface and then populate it with data from our data source. We then create an instance of the GreetingRules type and loop through the methods, calling the ones that match the expected signature.

▓ **Note**   We will go over how to make this discovery and dynamic invocation work in Chapter 6.

Automated Underwriting

Some of the most complex business rules you will find pop up in underwriting. This is true for mortgages, car loans, personal loans, and insurance of all kinds. When business groups start trying to manage risks, the business logic can easily get very complicated. We will need as much flexibility as we can get to handle the more nuanced business logic because these business rules can be complex and will change regularly.

Data Model

Let's start with an expression decision table and add some LoanCodes lookup data, as shown in Figure 3-2.

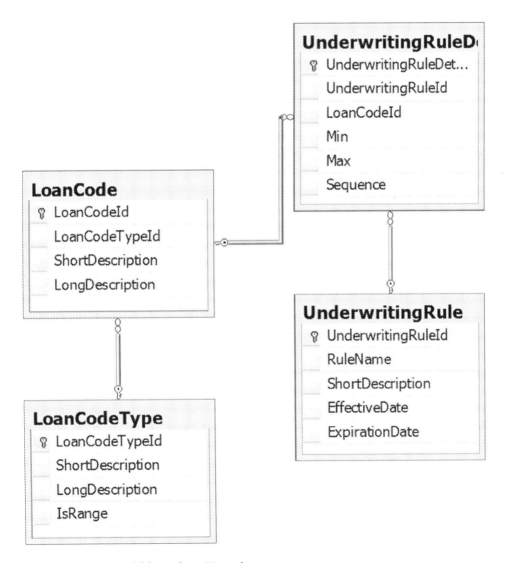

Figure 3-2. *Data model for underwriting rules*

In this data model, the `LoanCode` and `LoanCodeType` tables implement the OTLT anti-pattern. Ideally this should be kept separate from your transaction data to minimize the data integrity problems reviewed at the beginning of Chapter 2. The `UnderwritingRule` table defines the action for the rule and the `UnderwritingRuleDetail` table defines when a rule is applicable. These two tables collectively define our rule definitions. In this case, the "rules" will define an underwriting condition that must be satisfied prior to closing.

▓ **Note**   The `UnderwritingRule` table defines the action for the rule. In this case, the action will display messages to the users about conditions that need to be satisfied prior to closing. Often the `UnderwritingRule` may serve as the foreign key to additional "action" tables that define rate adjustments, loan product restrictions, optional coverage, LTV restrictions, etc. A single rule may serve as the trigger for any number of associated actions.

With this table structure, you can define a wide range of rules such as:

- Full doc requires two years bank statements for purchase of single family residence

- Full appraisal with three comps required for purchase

- Maximum LTV is 80% if the credit score is below 650 on a refinance unless the DTI is below 40%

▓ **Note**   These are not actual underwriting rules from any real mortgage company. The real rules may be much more confusing. In a real-life scenario there would be thousands of rules like these. Each of these rules may be updated with alarming regularity as the business adjusts to changes in the marketplace, to regulatory changes, and the actions of competitors.

Every industry is littered with its own acronyms. This is not unique to technobabble. The mortgage business is no different. Equally important to understanding the business logic is understanding the alphabet soup that can easily build up around these acronyms. In this case, LTV refers to Loan to Value ratio and DTI refers to Debt to Income ratio. While it is generally a best practice to spell out acronyms and not just assume that everyone knows them, some acronyms are so common that not using them may cause confusion, especially in translating logic to subject matter experts. FICO is another interesting example. A FICO score refers to your credit score. Most mortgage professionals are familiar with the term FICO score or credit score and may use them interchangeably, but few would understand what you mean by Fair Isaac Corporation, which is the base for the FICO acronym.

▓ **Tip**   You may also define underwriting rules in a composite pattern, where an underwriting rule could be defined as one or more underwriting rules plus its own definition. This would simplify defining and implementing underwriting rules because individual rules could be decomposed to their simplest form and common rules would not need to be repeated multiple times.

Now let's look at the data in these reference tables. The underwriting rule table will have three records listing the three rules identified earlier. Each rule will have a record in this table.

In looking at our sample rules, you will need 10 records in the LoanCodeType table. These will be:

- Documentation type
- Months of bank statements
- Loan purpose
- Property type
- Appraisal type
- Number of comps in appraisal
- Location
- DTI
- LTV
- Credit score

It's a little tougher to determine the number of records needed for the LoanCode table. You need a record for each possible value for each of the 10 LoanCodeType records you have identified. DTI, LTV, and credit score will be a little different. We will define these LoanCodeTypes as ranges, because the number of potential values would be overwhelming to state explicitly.

The interesting stuff happens in the UnderwritingRuleDetail table. This table will define the conditions that must be met in order for the business rule to apply. To interpret the logic in this table, we will start by selecting the records for a single rule and sorting by the Sequence column. As you work through the records, as long as the LoanCodeIds refer to the same LoanCodeTypeId, then the values will be joined through an OR expression. When a record refers to a new LoanCodeTypeId we create a new conditional statement. If the referenced LoanCodeType is a range, then you examine the Min and Max columns for the record and compare it to the corresponding property in the ILoanCodes object that will be passed to each rule. If the values for a loan pass all of the conditional tests, the BusinessRule is passed and you will display the associated message to the users, noting that the condition must be satisfied before the loan can close.

Data

To see how this fits together, let's plug in some actual data, as shown in Tables 3-5 through 3-8.

Underwriting Rule

Table 3-5. *Sample Data Naming the Underwriting Rules*

Underwriting Rule ID	Rule Name	Short Description
1	Full Doc Requirements	Full Doc requires two years bank statements for purchase of single family residence
2	Appraisal Requirements	Appraisal with three comps required for purchase
3	LTV Guideline	Maximum LTV is 80% if the Credit Score is below 650 on a refinance unless the DTI is below 40%

▓ **Tip**   In practice, you would most likely want to also include effective and expiration dates to maintain a history of what rules were in effect in the past. Many business scenarios require information about when the rate was locked, the policy bound, the employee hired, etc.

Loan Code Type

Table 3-6. *Sample Data Showing the Valid LoanCodeTypes Used in the OTLT*

Loan Code Type ID	Short Description	Long Description	Range
1	Documentation Type	Type of documentation used to verify income	0
2	Bank Statements	Number of months bank statements are available	0
3	Loan Purpose	Reason for this Loan	0
4	Property Type	Property type	0
5	Appraisal Type	Appraisal type	0
6	Comps	Number of comparable properties included in the appraisal	0
7	Location	Location	0
8	DTI	Debt to Income Ratio	1
9	LTV	Loan to Value Ratio	1
10	Credit Score	The middle credit score for the primary borrower	1

Loan Code

Table 3-7. *Sample Data Showing the Valid LoanCodeTypes and IDs*

Loan Code ID	Loan Code Type ID	Short Description
1	1	Full Doc
2	1	Lite Doc
3	1	No Doc
4	2	6 Months
5	2	12 Months
6	2	24 Months
7	3	Purchase
8	3	Cash Out Refinance
9	3	Debt Consolidation
10	4	Detached
11	4	Semi Detached
12	4	Townhome
13	4	Condo
14	4	Brownstone
15	5	Tax Appraisal
16	5	Market Comparison
17	5	Drive By Appraisal
18	5	Full Walk Through
19	6	1
20	6	2
21	6	3
22	7	Urban
23	7	Suburban
24	7	Rural
25	8	DTI
26	9	LTV
27	10	Credit Score

■ **Caution**   The actual values used here will probably be customer-specific and may change over time. You may see changes in how granular the business needs to track key values. A business may go from caring about the different reasons for refinancing to grouping all refinance loans together or they may decide to view all property types as single family or multi family. Depending on changes in the marketplace you may see the options grow or shrink for income documentation. Even items that seem to be set in stone should be viewed as potentially fluid.

Underwriting Rule Detail

Table 3-8. *The Detail Records to Define the First Underwriting Rule*

Underwriting Rule Detail ID	Underwriting Rule ID	Loan Code ID	Min	Max	Sequence
1	1	1	NULL	NULL	1
2	1	7	NULL	NULL	2
3	1	10	NULL	NULL	3
4	1	11	NULL	NULL	4
5	1	4	NULL	NULL	5
6	1	5	NULL	NULL	6
7	1	6	NULL	NULL	7

■ **Note**   This is only showing the details for the first business rules. Given the details for the other tables, you can fill in the blanks to see what the other rules would look like.

Code

We will start with the ILoanCode interface that will be passed to each rule (see Listing 3-4). This interface will expose properties for the loan code types defined in the LoanType table. In fact, we will be able to generate this interface based on the reference data in the LoanCodeType table.

Listing 3-4. Sample Implementation for the ILoanCode Interface

```
public interface ILoanCodes
{
    /// <summary>
    /// Type of documentation used to verify income
    /// </summary>
    int Code1 { get; set; }
    /// <summary>
    /// Number of Months Bank Statements are available
    /// </summary>
    int Code2 { get; set; }
    /// <summary>
```

```
    /// Reason for this Loan
    /// </summary>
    int Code3 { get; set; }
    /// <summary>
    /// Property Type
    /// </summary>
    int Code4 { get; set; }
    /// <summary>
    /// Appraisal Type
    /// </summary>
    int Code5 { get; set; }
    /// <summary>
    /// Number of comparable properties included in the appraisal
    /// </summary>
    int Code6 { get; set; }
    /// <summary>
    /// Location
    /// </summary>
    int Code7 { get; set; }
    /// <summary>
    /// Debt to Income Ratio
    /// </summary>
    decimal Code8 { get; set; }
    /// <summary>
    /// Loan to Value Ratio
    /// </summary>
    decimal Code9 { get; set; }
    /// <summary>
    /// The middle credit score for the primary borrower
    /// </summary>
    decimal Code10 { get; set; }
}
```

▪ **Tip** Depending on how volatile the `LoanCodeType` data is, you could also implement this interface as an array of tuples containing the `LoanCodeTypeId` and the `Value`. This may be more difficult to follow, but would be more resilient to change.

▪ **Tip** At the other end of the spectrum if the `LoanCodeType` data is fairly static, you could also implement the interface explicitly, naming each of the properties on the short description rather than the more generic `Code<LoanCodeTypeId>`. Because the interface definition and rule implementations are generated from the metadata, changing them is trivial, but any object implementing the interface would have to be updated whenever the interface's definition changes.

With the data that you defined for the first rule, you can implement it like Listing 3-5.

Listing 3-5. Implementation of the Business Rule Uses Positive Logic

```
/// <summary>
/// Full Doc requires 2 years Bank Statements for Purchase of Single Family Residence
/// </summary>
/// <param name="data">The loan codes to evaluate the rule against</param>
/// <returns></returns>
public bool Rule1(ILoanCodes data)
{
    var status = false;
    if (data.Code1 == 1)
    {
        if (data.Code3 == 7)
        {
            if (data.Code4 == 10 || data.Code4 == 11)
            {
                if (data.Code2 == 4 || data.Code4 == 5 || data.Code4 == 6)
                    status = true;
            }
        }
    }
    return status;
}
```

Or perhaps, you might prefer an implementation like Listing 3-6.

Listing 3-6. Implementation of the Business Rule Using Negative Logic

```
public bool Rule1(ILoanCodes data)
{
    if (data.Code1 != 1) return false;
    if (data.Code3 != 7) return false;
    if (data.Code4 != 10 && data.Code4 != 11) return false;
    if (data.Code2 == 4 || data.Code4 == 5 || data.Code4 == 6)
        return true;
    return false;
}
```

Both implementations are equivalent and we will explore how to generate either version. The second perhaps makes it clearer that if a loan fails any of the conditional tests, it is not subject to the business rule being defined.

▓ **Tip**   From this implementation, you can also see that you can get a slight optimization by putting the most restrictive requirements first, since the rule will fail as soon as one of the conditionals fails.

Summary

You saw what code based on the business logic in lookup tables looks like. You also saw a couple of guiding principles and best practices that should be adhered to, such as:

- You need an interface providing a property for each parameter in the decision table.

- If the rule passed, the return value should be populated with the details needed to implement the rule's action.

- If the rule did not pass, then the return value will often be null, empty, or false.

- Each method should have the same signature, making it easier to discover the rules at runtime.

- Based on your business logic and specific needs, you may need to run all rules and review the ones that passed, or you may be satisfied knowing that any rule passed and can stop evaluating rules as soon as you see one that passes.

So far, this discussion has been independent of any strategy for generating the code from the reference data. These best practices are still applicable regardless of how you create the logic. Now we will turn our attention to a specific strategy for generating the needed code. We will explore what Roslyn brings to the table and how to make the most of this new technology.

CHAPTER 4

An Introduction to Roslyn

Roslyn is the new compiler from Microsoft. It represents not only a rewrite of the compilers but also a reimagining of the compilation process in general. In the past, compiling code was a black box. Lines of code went in and a compiled assembly came out, or perhaps a slew of error messages. You could not interrupt this process to get access to any of the intermediate steps. All this changed with Roslyn. Figure 4-1 shows the steps Roslyn takes to compile code and identifies the APIs used to interact with the results at each stage.

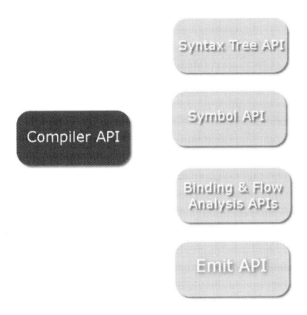

Figure 4-1. *The Roslyn pipeline*

The Roslyn Pipeline

With Roslyn, you can interrupt and interact with this process at various points along the way, as shown in the pipeline in Figure 4-1.

© Nick Harrison 2017
N. Harrison, *Code Generation with Roslyn*, DOI 10.1007/978-1-4842-2211-9_4

- Parsing is exposed through the syntax API. This will be the main driver for generating code.

- Symbols and metadata are exposed through the Symbol API and gives you the metadata on the code being compiled (more than you could dream of with reflection alone).

- Binding and flow analysis. API exposes the result of the compiler doing the semantic analysis of the code and can be helpful in understanding the inner workings of the code logic and dependencies.

- Emit API exposes the error messages if there are any, as well as the IL created for the assembly.

This opens up a lot of possibilities such as defining domain specific error messages, automating common refactors, flagging identified anti-patterns, and generating code. Code generation is what we are most interested in. As you will see, Roslyn gives you a great deal of control over the code that is generated and at the same time makes it substantially simpler than any of the strategies available in the past for generating code.

How Code Generation Fits In

Code generation strategies in the past were often based on running metadata through a template like T4 or structuring the code through objects in a library like the CodeDom. We won't even consider the painful prospect of dealing directly with StringBuilder to generate code, but not so long ago that may well have been your only option.

Many frameworks, such as Entity Framework and ASP.NET'S MVC Framework, use T4 to handle their code-generation needs. This gives the added advantage that you can simply change the template to influence the code that gets generated. T4 works well if the code being generated is very consistent and there is a clear pattern to follow, but template-based approaches do not lend themselves to dealing with complex conditional logic and the intricacies of business logic that would never be characterized as consistent.

CodeDom can handle complex business logic, but can be tedious to work with and maintain. It also shows its age. There is no support for advanced language features such as lambdas, anonymous types, auto properties, type initializers, etc. Even before these language features were added, there were core language features missing such as case statements and most of the looping structures. You could generally work around many of these constraints but it can get awkward.

Another common criticism frequently raised against the CodeDom was not being to reverse the process. You could easily generate code in any language given a CodeDom tree, but there was no mechanism for producing such a CodeDom tree from a given codebase.

■ **Note** One of the strongest selling points for the CodeDom was its language independence. Once you built a code generator with the CodeDom, you could generate the code in any DotNet language, but few people actually had a need to target multiple languages, and this feature was the source of many of CodeDom's limitations.

Building a code generator would be so much easier if we could start with sample code and get the CodeDom code needed to get the code you started with. We could then easily tweak it from there to get what we needed. Unfortunately this was never possible. So every Code Generator had to be built virtually from scratch. With CodeDom, this often felt like you were building a house and had to forge your own nails. It could get awkward and verbose.

Roslyn solves these problems. We get even greater control over the code that is generated than the CodeDom gave. The library used to express the code is the same objects that Roslyn uses while parsing the code. Automatically this means that we have full support for every language feature. Because the compiler uses these objects and we can intercept the compiler, we can now start with sample code and see what Roslyn does with it. We can start form this point and modify the code from there.

Getting Started with Roslyn

Let's start by creating a new solution. We will add a console application project to this project. Name this project Chapter 4. We will build the code for this chapter in this new project.

Run the following commands from the Package Manager Console in Visual Studio:

```
install-package Microsoft.CodeAnalysis      Install Language APIs and Services
```

After nuget works its magic, we will have all the references needed to interact with Roslyn, as shown in Figure 4-2.

Figure 4-2. *The Chapter 4 project with all the references added*

Syntax API

The first step in the compilation pipeline is parsing a string of source code into tokens in the target language. This can be keywords, identifiers, operators, etc. For example, the compiler may receive an input string like this:

```
a=b+c;
```

The compiler will parse this as an identifier a, an EqualsToken, an identifier b, a PlusToken, an identifier c, and a SemicolonToken.

■ **Note**   The parser actually goes into a lot more detail than this. The API is "full fidelity". Every character in the input will be represented in the resulting SyntaxTree, including whitespace, comments, etc. Because every character from the original input string is represented in the resulting syntax tree, this process is reversible. You can easily parse a string of code to get a SyntaxTree and then call the ToString() method on the SyntaxTree to get back to the original string. You can do this any number of times without losing any data or having any changes to the code in the end.

Once an input string has been parsed, you can call the ToString method on the SyntaxTree that was returned and get the original code. This reversibility is very valuable for code generation.

At this point, you don't have any semantic meaning and there is no context to understand how these tokens will interact and be used, but you can add your own tokens and nodes to the mix or swap out tokens or nodes to create the code that you want. Let's look at some sample code to start the compiler and interact with it at the end of the parsing stage.

Roslyn includes an abstract class that makes it easy to "visit" all of the nodes in a SyntaxTree. You can derive from the CSharpSyntaxWalker class to create your own walker to easily see what Roslyn knows about the code that you tell it to parse. Let's start with a Walker class that looks like Listing 4-1.

Listing 4-1. Walker Class to Walk the Nodes of the SyntaxTree

```
using Microsoft.CodeAnalysis;
using Microsoft.CodeAnalysis.CSharp;
using System;

namespace Chapter4
{
    public class Walker : CSharpSyntaxWalker
    {
        public Walker() : base(SyntaxWalkerDepth.StructuredTrivia)
        {
        }
        static int Tabs = 0;
        public override void Visit(SyntaxNode node)
        {
            Tabs++;
            var indents = new String(' ', Tabs * 3);
            Console.WriteLine(indents + node.Kind());
            base.Visit(node);
            Tabs--;
```

```
    }
    public override void VisitToken(SyntaxToken token)
    {
        var indents = new String(' ', Tabs * 3);
        Console.WriteLine(string.Format("{0}{1}:\t{2}", indents , token.Kind() , token));
        base.VisitToken(token);
    }
}
```

The base class defines a great many "visit" methods that could be overridden to handle visiting specific language structures. If you were particularly interested in Let clauses from LINQ queries, you could override the VisitLetClause method, as shown in Listing 4-2.

Listing 4-2. Overriding the VisitLetClause Method

```
public override void VisitLetClause(LetClauseSyntax node)
{
    Console.WriteLine("Found a let clause " + node.Identifier.Text);
    base.VisitLetClause(node);
}
```

▓ **Note**   You must override the base constructor and specify how deep you want to go in walking the code. Here, you indicate that you want to visit everything. The default is to only visit top-level declarations, which would not necessarily give you that much information. You don't actually do anything in the constructor except call the base constructor and specify how deep to go.

Every language structure has its own "visit" method that could potentially be overridden. You can parse some code and start the walker with a simple console application, as shown in Listing 4-3.

Listing 4-3. Calling the Walker on this Simple Code Snippet

```
using System;
using Microsoft.CodeAnalysis.CSharp;

namespace Chapter4
{
    class Program
    {
        static void Main(string[] args)
        {
            var tree = CSharpSyntaxTree.ParseText("a=b+c;");
            var walker = new Walker();
            walker.Visit(tree.GetRoot());
            Console.WriteLine("We can get back to the original code by call ToFullString ");
            Console.WriteLine(tree.GetRoot().ToFullString());
            Console.ReadLine();
        }
    }
}
```

When you run this code, you get the output shown in Listing 4-4.

Listing 4-4. Walking Simple Parsed Code

```
CompilationUnit
EndOfFileToken:
    SkippedTokensTrivia
    IdentifierToken:  a
    SkippedTokensTrivia
    EqualsToken:      =
    SkippedTokensTrivia
    IdentifierToken:  b
    SkippedTokensTrivia
    PlusToken:        +
    SkippedTokensTrivia
    IdentifierToken:  c
    SkippedTokensTrivia
    SemicolonToken:   ;
We can get back to the original code by call ToFullString
a=b+c;
```

Now extend this sample a little bit to parse some more realistic code. Parse the GreetingRules that you saw in Listing 3-2 from Chapter 3. For your reference, this code is also shown in Listing 4-5.

Listing 4-5. Implementation of the GreetingRule Class Shown in Chapter 3

```
public class GreetingRules

{
    public string Rule1(IGreetingProfile data)
    {
        if (data.Hour > 11) return null;
        if (data.Gender != 1) return null;

        return "Good Morning Mr. " + data.LastName;
    }

    public string Rule2(IGreetingProfile data)
    {
        if (data.Hour > 11) return null;
        if (data.Gender != 2) return null;
        if (data.MaritalStatus != 1) return null;
        return "Good Morning Mrs. " + data.LastName;
    }

    public string Rule3(IGreetingProfile data)
    {
        if (data.Hour > 11) return null;
        if (data.Gender != 2) return null;
        if (data.MaritalStatus != 2) return null;
        return "Good Morning Ms. " + data.LastName;
    }
```

```
    public string Rule4(IGreetingProfile data)
    {
        if (data.Hour < 12) return null;
        if (data.Hour < 17) return null;
        if (data.Gender != 1) return null;
        return "Good Afternoon Mr. " + data.LastName;
    }
}
```

You can parse this class and start the walker again with a simple console application, as shown in Listing 4-6.

Listing 4-6. Parsing the Greeting Rules from Listing 3-2 in Chapter 3

```
static void Main(string[] args)
{
    var code = "";
    using (var sr = new StreamReader("../../Code3_2.cs"))
    {
        code = sr.ReadToEnd();
    }
    var tree = CSharpSyntaxTree.ParseText(code);
    var walker = new Walker();
    walker.Visit(tree.GetRoot());
    Console.ReadLine();
}
```

░ **Note**   The StreamReader is simply reading the code that was shown in Listing 4-5. If you have that code stored somewhere else or want to parse some different code, simply change where the StreamReader is reading.

When you run the Walker over this sample rule, you get a lot of output. Parsed out into tokens, even a small simple sample code relies on the compiler tracking a lot of details (see Listing 4-7).

Listing 4-7. Sampling of the Walker Output from Parsing Listing 3-2

```
ClassDeclaration
PublicKeyword: public
ClassKeyword:  class
IdentifierToken:        GreetingRules
OpenBraceToken:         {
   MethodDeclaration
   PublicKeyword:       public
      PredefinedType
      StringKeyword:    string
   IdentifierToken:     Rule1
      ParameterList
      OpenParenToken:   (
         Parameter
```

```
        IdentifierName
          IdentifierToken:    IGreetingProfile
      IdentifierToken:     data
  CloseParenToken: )
  Block
  OpenBraceToken:  {
    IfStatement
    IfKeyword:     if
    OpenParenToken:        (
      GreaterThanExpression
        SimpleMemberAccessExpression
          IdentifierName
          IdentifierToken:     data
        DotToken:        .
          IdentifierName
          IdentifierToken:     Hour
      GreaterThanToken:  >
        NumericLiteralExpression
        NumericLiteralToken:    11
    CloseParenToken:      )
      ReturnStatement
      ReturnKeyword:     return
        NullLiteralExpression
        NullKeyword:     null
      SemicolonToken:     ;
```

■ **Note**   We will revisit parsing as we move forward. Being able to parse sample code and convert it to Roslyn objects is one of the features that gives Roslyn a substantial advantage over other code-generation strategies.

Symbol API

While the Syntax API is context free, the Symbol API will require some context to understand the various tokens that were parsed and apply meaning. The context that you will provide will includes a collection of SyntaxTrees, a collection of assembly references, and potentially compiler options.

■ **Note**   The output from the Syntax API becomes the input to the Symbol API. This is true for each step in the pipeline.

We can easily create the context needed using the Workspace API. Create an MSBuildWorkspace passing in the path to the solution file. The workspace will use the information from the solution file to create the context needed to access the compilation. Listing 4-8 shows how to set up this context and access the Compilation object.

Listing 4-8. Using the MSBuildWorkspace to Set Up the Context to Compile Chapter 3

```
using System;
using System.Linq;
using Microsoft.CodeAnalysis.MSBuild;

namespace Chapter4
{
    class Program
    {
        static void Main()
        {
            var work = MSBuildWorkspace.Create();
            var solution = work.OpenSolutionAsync(@"..\..\..\RoslynPlayGround.sln").Result;
            var project = solution.Projects.FirstOrDefault(p => p.Name == "Chapter3");
            if (project == null)
                throw new Exception("Could not find the Chapter 3 project");
            var compilation = project.GetCompilationAsync().Result;
            // Do something with the compilation
        }
    }
}
```

From a code generation perspective, you are most interested in using the Symbol API to get access to the metadata that can drive further code generation. The Symbol Table will give you access to reflection-like data from the source code as it is being compiled. Start by creating a new class called `Symbols`, as shown in Listing 4-9.

Listing 4-9. ReviewSymbolTable Explores some of the Data Exposed in the Symbol Table

```
using Microsoft.CodeAnalysis;
using Microsoft.CodeAnalysis.CSharp;
using Microsoft.CodeAnalysis.CSharp.Syntax;
using System;
using System.Collections.Generic;
using System.Linq;

namespace Chapter4
{
    public static class Symbols
    {
        public static void  ReviewSymbolTable(Compilation compilation)
        {
            foreach (var member in compilation.Assembly.GlobalNamespace.GetMembers( )
                .Where(member => member.CanBeReferencedByName))
            {
                Console.WriteLine(member.Name);
                foreach (var item in member.GetTypeMembers()
                    .Where(item => item.CanBeReferencedByName))
                {
                    Console.WriteLine("\t{0}:{1}", item.TypeKind, item.Name);
                    foreach (var innerItem in item.GetMembers()
```

```
                    .Where(innerItem => innerItem.CanBeReferencedByName))
                {
                    Console.WriteLine("\t\t{0}:{1}", innerItem.Kind, innerItem.Name);
                }
            }
        }
    }
}
```

Now you can update Listing 4-8 to call the ReviewSymbolTable method, as shown in Listing 4-10.

Listing 4-10. Calling the ReviewSymbolTable Method

```
using System;
using System.Linq;
using Microsoft.CodeAnalysis.MSBuild;

namespace Chapter4
{
    class Program
    {
        static void Main()
        {
            var work = MSBuildWorkspace.Create();

            var solution = work.OpenSolutionAsync(@"..\..\..\RoslynPlayGround.sln").Result;
            var project = solution.Projects.FirstOrDefault(p => p.Name == "Chapter3");
            if (project == null)
                throw new Exception("Could not find the Chapter 3 project");
            var compilation = project.GetCompilationAsync().Result;
            Symbols.ReviewSymbolTable(compilation);
            Console.ReadLine();
        }
    }
}
```

When you run the code from Listing 4-10, you get the output shown in Listing 4-11.

Listing 4-11. Viewing the Symbol Data Associated with the GreetingRules Class

```
Chapter3
        Enum:LoanPurpose
                Field:BusinessLaunching
                Field:HomePurchase
                Field:HomeImprovement
                Field:Investment
                Field:DebtConsolidation
                Field:Education
                Field:EmergencyExpendenture
                Field:CarPurchase
                Field:Wedding
                Field:Travel
```

```
Enum:Occupancy
        Field:OwnerOccupied
        Field:SecondHome
        Field:InvestmentProperty
Enum:PropertyTypes
        Field:DetachedHouse
        Field:SemiDetachedHouse
        Field:Townhome
        Field:Condominium
        Field:BrownStone
Class:GreetingRules
        Method:Rule1
        Method:Rule2
        Method:Rule3
        Method:Rule4
Interface:IGreetingProfile
        Property:Hour
        Property:Gender
        Property:MaritalStatus
        Property:FirstName
        Property:LastName
Class:GreetingProfile
        Property:FirstName
        Property:Gender
        Property:Hour
        Property:LastName
        Property:MaritalStatus
Interface:ILoanCodes
        Property:Code1
        Property:Code2
        Property:Code3
        Property:Code4
        Property:Code5
        Property:Code6
        Property:Code7
        Property:Code8
        Property:Code9
        Property:Code10
Class:Program
        Method:Main
Class:UnderwritingRules
        Method:Rule1
```

This is barely scratching the surface of the metadata that you now have at your disposal.

▨ **Note**   This will be very useful for using raw source code as metadata for future code generations.

Binding and Analysis API

As was the case with the Symbol API, the analysis APIs will depend on the step prior in the pipeline. So the `CSharpCompilation` that you created while exploring the symbols will become the source for driving the analysis details. The analysis step in the pipeline is referred to as *binding* because it takes into account everything that Roslyn knows about the code it is working on after binding the SyntaxTrees to symbols. Turns out it knows quite a bit.

You can unlock this fountain of information through the SemanticModel, which you get by passing a SyntaxTree to the `GetSemanticMethod` exposed by the `Compilation` object. Through the SemanticModel, the compiler spills the beans on everything that it has learned about how that SyntaxTree fits into the code being compiled.

You may often need to answer questions about the base type for a type declaration. You might often be interested in the metadata for a class once you know that it is derived from a specific class. You can use the SemanticModel to walk the inheritance tree and verify that this is a `TypeDeclaration` that we are interested in. Still working in the Symbols class you just created, add the `GetBaseClasses` static method shown in Listing 4-12.

Listing 4-12. Using SemanticModel to Get the Full Inheritance Hierarchy

```
public static IEnumerable<string> GetBaseClasses(SemanticModel model,
                    BaseTypeDeclarationSyntax type)
{
    var classSymbol = model.GetDeclaredSymbol(type);
    var returnValue = new List<INamedTypeSymbol>();
    while (classSymbol.BaseType != null)
    {
        returnValue.Add(classSymbol.BaseType);
        if (classSymbol.Interfaces != null)
            returnValue.AddRange(classSymbol.Interfaces);
        classSymbol = classSymbol.BaseType;
    }
    return returnValue;
}
```

This method will walk the inheritance tree back up to `System.Object` and return every interface implemented at each level. Using this method, you could easily filter to types that are derived from a specific type that you are interested in or implement a specific interface, as shown in Listing 4-13.

Listing 4-13. Finding the TypeDeclarationSyntax Derived from a Specific Class

```
public static IEnumerable<BaseTypeDeclarationSyntax>
    FindClassesDerivedOrImplementedByType(Compilation compilation, INamedTypeSymbol target)
{
    foreach (var tree in compilation.SyntaxTrees)
    {
        var semanticModel = compilation.GetSemanticModel(tree);

        foreach (var type in tree.GetRoot().DescendantNodes().OfType<TypeDeclarationSyntax>())
        {
            var baseClasses = GetBaseClasses(semanticModel, type);
            if (baseClasses != null)
                if (baseClasses.Contains(target))
```

```
            yield return type;
        }
    }
}

        var targetType = compilation.GetTypeByMetadataName("Chapter3.IGreetingProfile");
        var type = Symbols.FindClassesDerivedOrImplementedByType(compilation, targetType);
        Console.WriteLine(type.First().Identifier.ToFullString());
```

Emit API

With the Emit API, you can emit the assembly created by the compilation. This could either be to disk or a memory stream. You have full control over the output. Using the CompilationsOptions object, you can programmatically set and access every setting from a project's properties page, as well as the optimization level and platform.

While your code generator is being developed, you will also make heavy use of the diagnostics that is returned from calling Emit. The EmitResult object includes a property for success as well as a collection of diagnostics that provides access to the messages and the locations in the source code that had problems. Once your code generator is stable, this will become less relevant, but until then you will get very familiar with these objects.

■ **Note**   This diagnostic information is also available from several sources, including the SyntaxTree even before calling GetCompilation. Many diagnostics may not be found with a SyntaxTree without the symbol information creating through the compilation, but reviewing the diagnostics at every stage can still shed light on syntax errors while you are generating code.

Using the Workspace API, you can easily compile and emit the resulting assemblies, as shown in Listing 4-14.

Listing 4-14. Emitting the Results of the Compilation and Reviewing the Diagnostics

```
var solution = work.OpenSolutionAsync(@"..\..\..\RoslynPlayGround.sln").Result;
var project = solution.Projects.FirstOrDefault(p => p.Name == "Chapter3");
if (project == null)
    throw new Exception("Could not find the Chapter 3 project");
var compilation = project.GetCompilationAsync().Result;
var results = compilation.Emit("Chapter3.dll", "Chapter3.pdb");
if (!results.Success)
{
    foreach (var item in results.Diagnostics)
    {
        if (item.Severity == DiagnosticSeverity.Error)
        {
            Console.WriteLine(item.GetMessage());
        }
    }
}
```

If the emit results are not successful, then the two files you specified will be empty. You can apply various filters to the diagnostics to highlight the most relevant ones. The DiagnosticsSeverity will categorize each diagnostic as warning, error, information, or hidden. Each diagnostic also includes a property called IsWarningAsError so that you can track that a warning is being escalated to an error.

■ **Tip** As a best practice, strive to have no diagnostics reported in code that you generate.

Alternately, you may want to emit the results of the compilation to a MemoryStream and load the resulting assembly directly from memory without having to persist it to disk. Listing 4-15 shows an example of doing just this and then reporting on the methods found in the GreetingRules type.

Listing 4-15. Emitting the Assembly to Memory

```
var memory = new MemoryStream();
var results = compilation.Emit(memory);
var assembly = Assembly.Load(memory.ToArray());
var types   = assembly.GetTypes();
var greetingRules = types.FirstOrDefault(t => t.Name == "GreetingRules");
if (greetingRules == null)
    throw new Exception("Could not find the GreetingRules");
foreach (var rule in greetingRules.GetMethods(BindingFlags.Instance
                  | BindingFlags.DeclaredOnly
                  | BindingFlags.Public))
{
    Console.WriteLine(rule.Name);
}
```

■ **Tip** Loading an assembly from memory instead of disk allows you to avoid the potential of having a lock on an assembly, complicating future deployments.

Finally, you will probably want to explicitly give some compilation options. By default, you will get a debug build targeting any CPU. Most likely you will want a release build that targets a specific platform. Listing 4-16 shows an example that sets the most common compilation options.

Listing 4-16. Specifying Compilation Options for a Release Build on a 64-Bit Server

```
var options = new CSharpCompilationOptions(OutputKind.ConsoleApplication,
    optimizationLevel: OptimizationLevel.Release, platform: Platform.X64);
project = project.WithCompilationOptions(options);
var compilation = project.GetCompilationAsync().Result;
```

Generating Code

With this background information, you now know that generating code is simply a matter of adding the SyntaxNodes to the SyntaxTree that you are working on. You have a few options for how to do this. You have seen how CSharpSyntaxTree can be used to parse text and return a SyntaxTree. You can also use the CSharp. SyntaxFactory to create various SyntaxNodes and SyntaxTokens. Here, you will use both of these techniques to build a very simple code generator.

In the Chapter 4 project, create a new class and name it SimpleGenerator. Listing 4-17 shows the code you need to add to this class.

Listing 4-17. Create an Empty Class with the SimpleGenerator

```
public static SyntaxTree CreateEmptyClass(string className)
{
    var code = @"
        public class Class1
        {
        }
        ";
    var syntaxTree = CSharpSyntaxTree.ParseText(code);
    var identifierToken = syntaxTree.GetRoot().DescendantTokens()
        .First(t => t.IsKind(SyntaxKind.IdentifierToken)
                    && t.Parent.Kind() == SyntaxKind.ClassDeclaration);
    var newIdentifier = SyntaxFactory.Identifier(className);
    return SyntaxFactory.SyntaxTree(syntaxTree.GetRoot()
                .ReplaceToken(identifierToken, newIdentifier));
}
```

You start with a string literal to define a code snippet defining the skeleton for the class. This skeleton could be as simple or as complex as you want. Here, all you do is output the class name and assert that it will be public. Naturally, you probably do not want to name every class you generate Class1. To change the name for this class, you need to find the IdentifierToken responsible for giving the class its name. Listing 4-18 highlights how you can find this token.

Listing 4-18. Finding the IdentifierToken for the Class

```
var identifierToken = syntaxTree.GetRoot().DescendantTokens()
    .First(t => t.IsKind(SyntaxKind.IdentifierToken)
                && t.Parent.Kind() == SyntaxKind.ClassDeclaration);
```

You are looking for a token, not a node. This can cause a little bit of confusion because you will often be looking for nodes. Next you need to add some filters to ensure that you have the correct token. You need an IdentifierToken and you need it to be in a ClassDeclaration.

■ **Note** Without these checks in place, you could easily get the wrong token. Identifier tokens can be rather common.

Next you want to create a new identifier token with the desired name. This is shown in Listing 4-19.

Listing 4-19. Create a New Identifier Token

```
var newIdentifier = SyntaxFactory.Identifier(className);
```

Finally, you replace the old token with the new one, as shown in Listing 4-20.

Listing 4-20. Replace the Old Token with the New Token

```
return SyntaxFactory.SyntaxTree(syntaxTree.GetRoot()
            .ReplaceToken(identifierToken, newIdentifier));
```

Listing 4-21 shows you how to call this method and display the generated class.

Listing 4-21. Calling CreateEmptyClass and Displaying the Output

```
var emptyClassTree = SimpleGenerator.CreateEmptyClass("GreetingBusinessRule");
var emptyClass =
    emptyClassTree.GetRoot().DescendantNodes().
        OfType<ClassDeclarationSyntax>().FirstOrDefault();
if (emptyClass == null)
    return;
Console.WriteLine(emptyClass.NormalizeWhitespace().ToString());
```

Here, you search for the first `ClassDeclarationSyntax`, which will be the class that you just created. You should call the `NormalizeWhiteSpace` function on the `ClassDeclarationSyntax` before printing it so that the output will be nicely formatted for readability.

At this point, the generated class will look like what you see in Listing 4-22.

Listing 4-22. Current Version of the Generated Class

```
public class GreetingBusinessRule
{
}
```

Nothing too impressive yet, but you are just getting started. Now let's add a couple of properties to this new class. Listing 4-23 shows some code that can be used to add a property.

Listing 4-23. Adding a Property to the Generated Class

```
public static ClassDeclarationSyntax AddProperty(this ClassDeclarationSyntax currentClass,
    string name,INamedTypeSymbol type)
{
    if (currentClass.DescendantNodes().OfType<PropertyDeclarationSyntax>()
        .Any(p => p.Identifier.Text == name))
    {
        // class already has the specified property
        return currentClass;
    }
    var typeSentax = SyntaxFactory.ParseTypeName(type.Name);
    var newProperty = SyntaxFactory.PropertyDeclaration(typeSentax, name)
        .WithModifiers(
            SyntaxFactory.TokenList(
                SyntaxFactory.Token(SyntaxKind.PublicKeyword)))
        .WithAccessorList(
            SyntaxFactory.AccessorList(
                SyntaxFactory.List(
                    new[]
```

```
        {
            SyntaxFactory.AccessorDeclaration(SyntaxKind.GetAccessorDeclaration)
                .WithSemicolonToken(SyntaxFactory.Token(SyntaxKind.SemicolonToken)),
            SyntaxFactory.AccessorDeclaration(SyntaxKind.SetAccessorDeclaration)
                .WithSemicolonToken(SyntaxFactory.Token(SyntaxKind.SemicolonToken))
        })));
    return currentClass.AddMembers(newProperty);
}
```

The first thing to note is that this method is defined as an extension method to the ClassDeclarationSyntax object. This is not strictly necessary, but it does allow the method to participate nicely in the method chaining process. Another subtle point to consider is the first conditional statement in the method. Here, you check to see if the class already has a property with the same name. If it does, you simply ignore it and return the original class unchanged. You may want to also check by matching against type or even throw an exception if there is a match. You may also want to consider adding a call to Count(). That way, you can count the properties and then throw an exception if the class already has too many properties (see Listing 4-24).

Listing 4-24. Complain if Too Many Properties Are Added to the Class

```
if (currentClass.DescendantNodes().OfType<PropertyDeclarationSyntax>().Count() > 128)
    throw new Exception("Class already has too many properties");
```

■ **Note** The 128 cutoff value used in Listing 4-24 is arbitrary. The actual upper bound for properties in a class is in the millions, but good design advises you to cut it off well before then.

This method can be a bit more complicated because you have to provide an INamedTypeSymbol for the second parameter. The easiest way to get an INamedTypeSymbol is through the Compilation object. This seems a little bit counterintuitive because you are generating code, not compiling, but the Compilation object has the context to properly specify the details for the INamedTypeSymbol. Let's start by creating the Compilation object and giving it the context that you need, as shown in Listing 4-25.

Listing 4-25. Create a Compilation with the Context to CreateINamedTypeSymbols

```
var reference = MetadataReference.CreateFromFile(typeof (object).Assembly.Location);
var compilation = CSharpCompilation.Create("internal")
    .WithReferences(reference);
```

■ **Note** The context provided in Listing 4-25 is a reference to the assembly where System.Object is defined.

Now you can create your types, as shown in Listing 4-26.

Listing 4-26. Creating the INamedTypeSymbols for Your Properties

```
var intType = compilation.GetTypeByMetadataName("System.Int32");
var stringType = compilation.GetTypeByMetadataName("System.String");
var dateTimeType = compilation.GetTypeByMetadataName("System.DateTime");
```

Now add some properties to the class, as shown in Listing 4-27.

Listing 4-27. Adding Properties to the Class and Displaying the New Class

```
emptyClass = emptyClass.AddProperty("Age", intType)
                .AddProperty("FirstName", stringType)
                .AddProperty("LastName", stringType)
                .AddProperty("DateOfBirth", dateTimeType)
                .NormalizeWhitespace();
Console.WriteLine(emptyClass.ToString());
```

At this point, this class is looking a bit more impressive, as you can see in Listing 4-28.

Listing 4-28. The Generated Class with Properties

```
public class GreetingBusinessRule
{
    public Int32 Age
    {
        get;
        set;
    }

    public String FirstName
    {
        get;
        set;
    }

    public String LastName
    {
        get;
        set;
    }

    public DateTime DateOfBirth
    {
        get;
        set;
    }
}
```

We have only scratched the surface of code generation, but we introduced some patterns that you will see applied throughout any code generation initiative you undertake. We will explore these and more strategies more fully in Chapter 5.

Summary

Roslyn is a big topic. It is substantially different than the view typically taken when building a compiler and exposing the inner workings of the compiler. This chapter touched on many of the core concepts and components of Roslyn. There is still much that we have not explored simply because it does not relate to code generation.

This chapter reviewed the Roslyn pipeline and the steps Roslyn takes while compiling code. You saw how to intercept each of these steps and interact with the internals of Roslyn. At each step, the chapter focused on the implications from a code generation perspective. In many cases, code generation is at best a happy side effect of the true goal that the Roslyn designers had in mind.

In Chapter 5, we will expand on how to generate code with Roslyn. You will see new ways to generate code and new ways to structure your code generators. You will also learn how to generate the code that you looked at in Chapter 3 when we discussed pulling table-driven logic into code.

Generating Code

So far we have explored the benefits of moving business logic from application code to reference data in the database. You saw how hand-coding business rules in your application logic can lead to brittle code that's not resilient to change. At the very least, this code can leave you less responsive to changes in the marketplace, which could leave you out of the marketplace all together. We then explored various strategies for storing different types of business rules in variations on a standard decision table.

We then turned our attention to what it might look like if we implemented these table-driven business rules in code. As explained in Chapter 1, we still don't want to hand-write these business rules manually; letting the computer write the business rules will allow you to bypass the problems you saw in Chapter 1. In Chapter 4, we surveyed Roslyn to get a feel for how its various components fit together. You saw that among other things, Roslyn is well positioned to allow you to roughly describe the business rules and then fill in the gaps with details from the decision tables holding your business rules. This can allow you to have the best of both worlds—the speed of compiled code and the maintenance ease of table-driven logic.

Creating Enums

Any lookup table in the database can be treated as an Enum in your code. In Chapter 2, you saw a couple of different variations for structuring lookup tables. In a transaction system, you would typically want a separate table for each lookup type to get the best support for data integrity. For a rules engine or reporting database that's less tied to referential integrity, you may find some lookup tables (or even all) grouped together as an OTLT (One True Lookup Table). Regardless of the original source, the resulting enums will generally follow a common structure. There is, after all, not very many ways that enums can differ. See Listing 5-1.

Listing 5-1. A Simple Enum

```
public enum Occupancy
{
    [Description("Owner Occupied")]
    OwnerOccupied = 1
}
```

▓ **Caution** Although enums are very simple, creating one can be more cumbersome than you might initially think, especially when you want to incorporate as much metadata as possible into the resulting code structure.

When working with Roslyn, you will discover that every part of your code has a name and is represented by a specific data type in the SyntaxTree. Think about diagramming sentences from grammar class. This may seem cumbersome, but it allows you to be very precise in structuring and manipulating code. Starting with the first line from Listing 5-1, we have an EnumDeclaration modified with the Public keyword token and named Occupancy. Lines 2 and 5 are simply the OpenBraceToken and CloseBraceToken, respectively. Line 4 is an EnumMemberDeclaration and Line 3 is an attribute attached to the EnumMemberDeclaration. The EnumMemberDeclaration also includes an EqualsValueClause where you can explicitly assign the member a value. That are a lot components for such a simple structure.

Looking back at Table 3-7, you can easily see where the data would come from to fill in the details for the enum. For every record in the LoanCodeType table, we will have an EnumDeclaration. The name for the Enum comes from the Short Description column. For each matching record in the LoanCode table, we define an EnumMemberDeclaration. The name comes from the Short Description, the value being assigned to the EnumMember comes from the Loan Code ID column, and the AttributeArgument passed to the DescriptionAttribute comes from Long Description column.

You can pull these relevant details together into simple objects—EnumTypeItem and EnumTypeDetailItem (see Listing 5-2).

Listing 5-2. Container Objects for Enum Details

```
public class EnumTypeItem
{
    public string ShortDescription { get; set; }
    public string LongDescription { get; set; }
    public bool IsRange { get; set; }
    public int Id { get; set; }
}
public class EnumTypeDetailItem
{
    public int LoanCodeId { get; set; }
    public int LoanCodeTypeId { get; set; }
    public string ShortDescription { get; set; }
    public string LongDescription { get; set; }
}
```

▓ **Tip** Creating such simple objects to hold the metadata for code generation will help keep the metadata separate from the code generation and will make the code generation logic simpler since it doesn't have to worry about getting and mapping the metadata.

You can populate these types with a couple of simple SQL queries, as shown in Listing 5-3.

Listing 5-3. Populating EnumDetail

```
public static IList<EnumTypeItem> GetEnumData(Database database)
{
    if (database == null) throw new Exception("Playground database was not found ");
    var sql = @"SELECT
                LoanCodeTypeId,
                ShortDescription,
                LongDescription,
```

```
                IsRange
             FROM dbo.LoanCodeType";
var data = database.ExecuteWithResults(sql);
var table = data.Tables[0];
var enumTypes = new List<EnumTypeItem>();
foreach (DataRow record in table.Rows)
{
    var item = (new EnumTypeItem
    {
        Id = (int)record[0],
        ShortDescription = (string)record[1],
        LongDescription = (string)record[2],
        IsRange = (bool)record[3],
        Details = new List<EnumTypeDetailItem>()
    });
    sql = @"SELECT  LoanCodeId ,
                   LoanCodeTypeId ,
                   ShortDescription ,
                   ISNULL(LongDescription, '')
            FROM   LoanCode
            WHERE  LoanCodeTypeId = " + record[0].ToString();
    var details = database.ExecuteWithResults(sql);
    foreach (DataRow row in details.Tables[0].Rows)
    {
        item.Details.Add(new EnumTypeDetailItem
        {
            LoanCodeId = (int)row[0],
            LoanCodeTypeId = item.Id,
            LongDescription = (string)row[3],
            ShortDescription = (string)row[2]
        });
    }
    enumTypes.Add(item);
}
return enumTypes;
}
```

▓ **Note**   This code uses the SMO (SQL Server Management Objects) library to get the metadata. You can use whatever data access logic you are most comfortable with.

Now that you have the relevant details and know where they go, you are ready to generate some code. There are a couple of different approaches that you could follow. One example relies on parsing sample code and then manipulating the SyntaxNodes in the resulting SyntaxTree to get the result that you want. The other approach relies on building up the code you want piece by piece using the SyntaxFactory. The SyntaxFactory has a method for creating the appropriate SyntaxNode for every language construct.

C# syntax is generally unambiguous. There is generally only one way for the ParseText to build a SyntaxTree so only a few assumptions have to be made. However, because everything is strongly typed with the SyntaxFactory approach, you will have the most control over the final SyntaxTree. Some performance tests show the ParseText approach to be more performant. This is most likely the result of optimizations internal to Roslyn.

57

> ▓ **Tip** You will hear people argue in favor of one approach or the other. In the end, use the approach you are most comfortable with. Here we will use a mix of both approaches, starting with some sample code but using the SyntaxFactory as needed.

We will start with some text to parse, as shown in Listing 5-4.

Listing 5-4. Creating the Initial SyntaxTree

```
var code = @"
[EnumDescription("" "")]
public enum EnumName
{
   [MemberDescription ("" "")]
   Name = Value;
}";
var syntaxTree = CSharpSyntaxTree.ParseText(code);
```

> ▓ **Note** The SyntaxTree in Listing 5-4 will serve as the basis for each of the enums. As you loop through the list of EnumTypeItems, we refer to this SyntaxTree.

The main process here will be to find the relevant nodes that you want to manipulate and replace key details with data from the metadata. You can start by filling in the details for the EnumDescription attribute if there is an actual value for the LongDescription (see Listing 5-5).

Listing 5-5. Adding a DescriptionAttribute to the Enum

```
var newSyntaxTree = syntaxTree.GetRoot();
if (!string.IsNullOrEmpty(data.LongDescription))
{
    var literal = newSyntaxTree.DescendantNodes()
        .OfType<LiteralExpressionSyntax>().FirstOrDefault();
    var newLiteral = SyntaxFactory.LiteralExpression
        (SyntaxKind.StringLiteralExpression,
        SyntaxFactory.Literal(data.LongDescription));
    newSyntaxTree = newSyntaxTree.ReplaceNode(literal,
        newLiteral);
}
else
{
    var attribute = newSyntaxTree.DescendantNodes()
        .OfType<AttributeSyntax>().FirstOrDefault();
    if (attribute != null)
        newSyntaxTree = newSyntaxTree.RemoveNode
            (attribute, SyntaxRemoveOptions.KeepNoTrivia);
}
```

If you have a `LongDescription` to put in the `EnumDescription` attribute, you find the `LiteralExpressionSyntax` associated with the parameter and replace it with a new Literal. If there is no `LongDescription` available, you find the `AttributeSyntax` and remove it from the SyntaxTree. Next, we will want to fill in the true name for the enum. To do this, you need to find the IdentifierToken for the `EnumDeclaration` and replace it with a new identifier with the name of the enum, as shown in Listing 5-6.

Listing 5-6. Renaming the Enum

```
var identifierToken = newSyntaxTree.DescendantTokens()
    .First(t => t.IsKind(SyntaxKind.IdentifierToken)
                && t.Parent.Kind() == SyntaxKind.EnumDeclaration);
var newIdentifier = SyntaxFactory.Identifier
    (data.ShortDescription.Replace(" ", ""));
newSyntaxTree = SyntaxFactory.SyntaxTree
    (newSyntaxTree.ReplaceToken(identifierToken, newIdentifier)).GetRoot();
```

▓ **Tip**   Here we strip out the whitespace in the Short Description if there is any to get a valid name for the enum. Depending on your data and your needs, you may need additional data scrubs to come up with good names for your `enum`s.

Now you are ready to loop through the `EnumTypeItem.Details` and add the members to the enum. Start by finding the `EnumMemberDeclarationSyntax` from the original SyntaxTree and then modify the member declaration by renaming it, as shown in Listing 5-7.

Listing 5-7. Renaming the Enum Member

```
var memberDeclaration = newSyntaxTree.DescendantNodes()
    .OfType<EnumMemberDeclarationSyntax>()
    .FirstOrDefault();
memberDeclaration = memberDeclaration.WithIdentifier
  (SyntaxFactory.Identifier(item.ShortDescription
        .Replace(" ", "")));
```

You also need to explicitly set the value for the enum item, as shown in Listing 5-8.

Listing 5-8. Assigning a Value to the Enum Member

```
memberDeclaration = memberDeclaration.
    WithEqualsValue(SyntaxFactory
    .EqualsValueClause(SyntaxFactory.LiteralExpression
    (SyntaxKind.NumericLiteralExpression,
    SyntaxFactory.Literal(item.LoanCodeId))));
```

Now you are ready to turn your attention to the `MemberDescription` attribute. If you have a Long Description, you want to add it to the description. If you don't have a Long Description, go ahead and remove the attribute all together. Either way, start by finding the attribute. See Listing 5-9.

Listing 5-9. Adding a Description Attribute to the Enum Member

```
var attributeDeclaration =
    memberDeclaration.DescendantNodes()
    .OfType<AttributeListSyntax>()
    .FirstOrDefault();
if (!string.IsNullOrEmpty(item.LongDescription))
{
    var description =
      attributeDeclaration.DescendantNodes()
        .OfType<LiteralExpressionSyntax>()
        .FirstOrDefault();
    var newDescription = SyntaxFactory.LiteralExpression
        (SyntaxKind.StringLiteralExpression,
            SyntaxFactory.Literal(item.LongDescription));
    var newAttribute = attributeDeclaration.ReplaceNode
        (description, newDescription);
    memberDeclaration = memberDeclaration.ReplaceNode
        (attributeDeclaration, newAttribute);
}
else
{
    memberDeclaration = memberDeclaration.RemoveNode
        (attributeDeclaration,
            SyntaxRemoveOptions.KeepNoTrivia);
}
```

■ **Caution**   Always remember that Roslyn objects are immutable. You must keep track of the return values from function calls and incorporate the new objects back into the SyntaxTree, otherwise any changes you make will be lost.

Once you have processed all the details from the EnumTypeItem, you should clean up and remove the first member that you used as the starting point:

```
var firstMember = newSyntaxTree.DescendantNodes()
        .OfType<EnumMemberDeclarationSyntax>().FirstOrDefault();
newSyntaxTree = newSyntaxTree.RemoveNode(firstMember, SyntaxRemoveOptions.KeepNoTrivia);
```

■ **Note**   Enums are harder to generate than you would expect because of the conditional attributes to provide additional metadata about the enum and its values, but providing this data in the generated code is well worth the extra effort.

Running this code against the LoanCodeType and LoanCode tables that you saw at the end of Chapter 3 will generate the enums shown in Listing 5-10.

Listing 5-10. Generated Enums

```
[EnumDescription("Type of documentation used to verify income")]
public enum DocumentationType
{
    [MemberDescription("Full Documentation")]
    FullDoc = 2,
    [MemberDescription("Lite Documentation")]
    LiteDoc = 3,
    [MemberDescription("No Documentation")]
    NoDoc = 4
}
[EnumDescription("Number of Months Bank Statements available")]
public enum BankStatements
{
    [MemberDescription("Six Months")]
    SixMonths = 5,
    [MemberDescription("Twelve Months")]
    TwelveMonths = 6,
    [MemberDescription("Twenty Four Months")]
    TwentyFourMonths = 7
}
[EnumDescription("Reason for this loan")]
public enum LoanPurpose
{
    [MemberDescription("Purchase")]
    Purchase = 8,
    [MemberDescription("Cash Our Refinance")]
    CashOurRefinance = 9,
    [MemberDescription("Debt Consolidation")]
    DebtConsolidation = 10
}
[EnumDescription("Property Type")]
public enum PropertyType
{
    [MemberDescription("Detached")]
    Detached = 11,
    [MemberDescription("Semi Detached")]
    SemiDetached = 12,
    [MemberDescription("Townhome")]
    Townhome = 13,
    [MemberDescription("Condo")]
    Condo = 14,
    [MemberDescription("Brownstone")]
    Brownstone = 15
}
[EnumDescription("Appraisal Type")]
public enum AppraisalType
{
    [MemberDescription("Tax Appraisal")]
    TaxAppraisal = 16,
    [MemberDescription("Market Comparison")]
    MarketComparison = 17,
```

```
    [MemberDescription("Drive By Appraisal")]
    DriveByAppraisal = 18,
    [MemberDescription("Full Walk Through")]
    FullWalkThrough = 19
}
[EnumDescription("Number of comparable properties included in the appraisal")]
public enum Comps
{
    [MemberDescription("One Comp")]
    OneComp = 20,
    [MemberDescription("Two Comps")]
    TwoComps = 21,
    [MemberDescription("Three Comps")]
    ThreeComps = 22
}
[EnumDescription("Location")]
public enum Location
{
    [MemberDescription("Urban")]
    Urban = 23,
    [MemberDescription("Suburban")]
    Suburban = 24,
    [MemberDescription("Rural")]
    Rural = 25
}
```

Hello World

Now let's turn our attention back to the GreetingRules from Chapter 3. For your reference, the rules defined there are repeated in Table 5-1.

Table 5-1. *Greeting Rule Definitions*

Greeting Rule ID	HourMin	HourMax	Gender	Marital Status	Greeting
1	NULL	11	1	NULL	Good Morning Mr.
2	NULL	11	2	1	Good Morning Mrs.
3	NULL	11	2	2	Good Morning Ms.
4	12	17	1	NULL	Good Afternoon Mr.
5	12	17	2	1	Good Afternoon Mrs.
6	12	17	2	2	Good Afternoon Ms.
7	18	22	1	NULL	Good Evening Mr.
8	18	22	2	1	Good Evening Mrs.
9	18	22	2	2	Good Evening Ms.
10	23	NULL	1	NULL	Good Night Mr.
11	23	NULL	2	1	Good Night Mrs.
12	23	NULL	2	2	Good Night Mrs.

As discussed in Chapter 3, these rules can be implemented with the logic shown in Listing 5-11.

Listing 5-11. Sample Implementation of the Greeting Rules

```
public class GreetingRules
    {
        public string Rule1(IGreetingProfile data)
        {
            if (data.Hour > 11) return null;
            if (data.Gender != 1) return null;
            return "Good Morning Mr. " + data.LastName;
        }

        public string Rule2(IGreetingProfile data)
        {
            if (data.Hour > 11) return null;
            if (data.Gender != 2) return null;
            if (data.MaritalStatus != 1) return null;
            return "Good Morning Mrs. " + data.LastName;
        }

        public string Rule3(IGreetingProfile data)
        {
            if (data.Hour > 11) return null;
            if (data.Gender != 2) return null;
            if (data.MaritalStatus != 2) return null;
            return "Good Morning Ms. " + data.LastName;
        }

        public string Rule4(IGreetingProfile data)
        {
            if (data.Hour < 12) return null;
            if (data.Hour < 17) return null;
            if (data.Gender != 1) return null;
            return "Good Afternoon Mr. " + data.LastName;
        }
}
```

▓ **Note** This is a sampling of the rules implied by the lookup data. The rest of the rules have been left out for the sake of brevity.

To simplify the logic and the code needed to generate the code, we will invert all the conditional statements implied in the rule definition. Instead of testing to ensure that the IGreetingProfile parameter's data meets all of the criteria, we will check all of the ways that the IGreetingProfile could fail a criteria and immediately return null if any condition is not met. The most direct and intuitive approach for implementing GreetingRule1 may look like Listing 5-12.

Listing 5-12. Direct Literal Interpretation of a Greeting Rule

```
public string Rule1(IGreetingProfile data)
{
    if ((data.Hour <= 11) && (data.Gender == 1))
        return "Good Morning Mr. " + data.LastName;
    else return null;
}
```

This takes a direct and literal interpretation of the reference data, but by inverting the conditionals, you can end up with a simpler implementation, as shown in Listing 5-13.

Listing 5-13. Streamlined Implementation Based on Inverting the Logic

```
public string Rule1(IGreetingProfile data)
{
    if (data.Hour > 11) return null;
    if (data.Gender != 1) return null;
    return "Good Morning Mr. " + data.LastName;
}
```

Regardless of the number of conditionals and their relative complexities, this second approach will allow you to avoid all nested conditionals and bypass compound conditionals.

░ **Tip**   This will make a code generator easier to write, easier to follow, and less likely to have logic errors in the generator.

As you did with the enums, you start with a simple object used to hold the details of a GreetingRule, as shown in Listing 5-14.

Listing 5-14. Simple Object for Holding the GreetingRule Metadata

```
public class GreetingRuleDetail
{
    public int GreetingRuleId { get; set; }
    public int? HourMin { get; set; }
    public int? HourMax { get; set; }
    public int? Gender { get; set; }
    public int? MaritalStatus { get; set; }
    public string Greeting { get; set; }
}
```

░ **Note**   Most of these properties are nullable, reflecting the data model. If no value is specified for a given property, that property will not be a factor in the rule evaluation.

We will use this plus the IGreetingProfile from Chapter 3, as shown in Listing 5-15.

Listing 5-15. IGreetingProfile Passed to Every Greeting Rule Being Evaluated

```
public interface IGreetingProfile
    {
        int Hour { get; set; }
        int Gender { get; set; }
        int MaritalStatus { get; set; }
        string FirstName { get; set; }
        string LastName { get; set; }
    }
```

To generate the code, start by running a simple query to get the details. Once you have these details, you loop through the GreetingRuleDetail items and create a new method for each item. Because of how we simplified the logic, you can treat each criteria individually and simply add a condition for each criteria that has a value (see Listing 5-16).

Listing 5-16. The Main Driver for Generating Greeting Rules

```
var code = @"public class GreetingRules{}";
var method = @"public string Rule(IGreetingProfile data){}";
var syntaxTree = CSharpSyntaxTree.ParseText(code).GetRoot();
var methodSyntaxTree = CSharpSyntaxTree.ParseText(method)
    .GetRoot();
var classDeclaration = syntaxTree.DescendantNodes()
    .OfType<ClassDeclarationSyntax>()
    .FirstOrDefault();
var originalDeclaration = classDeclaration;
foreach (var rule in GetGreetingRuleDetails())
{
    var greetingRule = methodSyntaxTree.DescendantNodes()
        .OfType<MethodDeclarationSyntax>()
        .FirstOrDefault();
    var identifierToken = greetingRule.DescendantTokens()
        .First(t => t.IsKind(SyntaxKind.IdentifierToken)
            && t.Parent.Kind() == SyntaxKind.MethodDeclaration);
    var newIdentifier = SyntaxFactory.Identifier
        ("Rule" + rule.GreetingRuleId);
    greetingRule = greetingRule
        .ReplaceToken(identifierToken, newIdentifier);
    if (rule.HourMin.HasValue)
    {
        var newBlock = ProcessHourCondition(rule.HourMin.Value,
            greetingRule.Body, SyntaxKind.LessThanExpression);
        greetingRule = greetingRule.WithBody(newBlock);
    }
    if (rule.HourMax.HasValue)
    {
        var newBlock = ProcessHourCondition(rule.HourMax.Value,
            greetingRule.Body, SyntaxKind.GreaterThanExpression);
        greetingRule = greetingRule.WithBody(newBlock);
    }
```

```
    if (rule.Gender.HasValue)
    {
        var newBlock = ProcessEqualityComparison("Gender",
            rule.Gender.Value, greetingRule.Body);
        greetingRule = greetingRule.WithBody(newBlock);
    }
    if (rule.MaritalStatus.HasValue)
    {
        var newBlock = ProcessEqualityComparison("MaritalStatus",
            rule.MaritalStatus.Value, greetingRule.Body);
        greetingRule = greetingRule.WithBody(newBlock);
    }
    var currentBlock = AddRuleReturnValue
        (greetingRule.Body,  rule);
    greetingRule = greetingRule.WithBody(currentBlock);
    classDeclaration = classDeclaration.AddMembers(greetingRule);
}
```

This shows you the general structure for generating the rules, but most of the details are in the helper methods ReturnNull, AddRuleReturnValue, ProcessHourCondition, and ProcessEqualityComparison. These methods allow you to reuse a lot of logic as well as make the structure of your logic more visible.

Let's start with the simplest. ReturnNull will produce a ReturnStatementSyntax with a literal null, as shown in Listing 5-17.

Listing 5-17. The ReturnNull Helper Method

```
private static ReturnStatementSyntax ReturnNull()
{
    return SyntaxFactory.ReturnStatement
      (SyntaxFactory.LiteralExpression(
            SyntaxKind.NullLiteralExpression));
}
```

AddRuleReturnValue is a little bit more complicated. Here, you need to generate code to look like this:

```
return "Good Morning Mr. " + data.LastName;
```

with the string literal coming from the rule.Greeting. Each method will return this value if none of the internal tests fails, as shown in Listing 5-18.

Listing 5-18. Code to Return the Successful Return Value from the Rule

```
private static BlockSyntax AddRuleReturnValue
      (BlockSyntax currentBlock, GreetingRuleDetail rule)
{
    var ruleGreeting = SyntaxFactory.LiteralExpression
        (SyntaxKind.StringLiteralExpression,
            SyntaxFactory.Literal(rule.Greeting));
    var lastName = SyntaxFactory.MemberAccessExpression
        (SyntaxKind.SimpleMemberAccessExpression,
            SyntaxFactory.IdentifierName("data"),
        SyntaxFactory.IdentifierName("LastName"));
```

```
        var assignment = SyntaxFactory.BinaryExpression
                (SyntaxKind.AddExpression, ruleGreeting, lastName);
    var returnStatement = SyntaxFactory.ReturnStatement(assignment);
    return currentBlock.AddStatements(new StatementSyntax[]
            { returnStatement });
}
```

Because you pass in the comparison type, you can use the same method to handle min hour and the max hour comparisons. Listing 5-19 shows how you can invert the logic.

Listing 5-19. ProcessHourCondition

```
ProcessHourCondition(rule.HourMin.Value, greetingRule.Body, SyntaxKind.LessThanExpression);
ProcessHourCondition(rule.HourMax.Value, greetingRule.Body, SyntaxKind.
GreaterThanExpression);

        private static BlockSyntax ProcessHourCondition(int hourValue,
            BlockSyntax currentBlock, SyntaxKind comparisonType)
        {
            var hourExpression = SyntaxFactory.MemberAccessExpression(
                    SyntaxKind.SimpleMemberAccessExpression,
                    SyntaxFactory.IdentifierName("data"),
                    SyntaxFactory.IdentifierName("Hour"));
            var condition = SyntaxFactory.BinaryExpression(comparisonType,
                    hourExpression,
                    SyntaxFactory.LiteralExpression(
                            SyntaxKind.NumericLiteralExpression,
                            SyntaxFactory.Literal(hourValue)));
            var newConditional = SyntaxFactory.IfStatement(
                                condition,ReturnNull());
            return currentBlock.AddStatements(new StatementSyntax[] {
                    newConditional });
        }
```

For the `Gender` and `MaritalStatus` parameters, you can reuse the same evaluation logic by passing in the parameter from the `IGreetingProfile` that you want to test, as shown in Listing 5-20.

Listing 5-20. ProcessEqualityComparison

```
private static BlockSyntax ProcessEqualityComparison
    (string whichEquality, int value, BlockSyntax currentBlock)
{
    var genderReference = SyntaxFactory.MemberAccessExpression(
        SyntaxKind.SimpleMemberAccessExpression,
        SyntaxFactory.IdentifierName("data"),
        SyntaxFactory.IdentifierName(whichEquality));
    var condition = SyntaxFactory.BinaryExpression
        (SyntaxKind.NotEqualsExpression,
         genderReference, SyntaxFactory.LiteralExpression(
         SyntaxKind.NumericLiteralExpression,
         SyntaxFactory.Literal(value)));
```

```
    var newConditional = SyntaxFactory.IfStatement(condition,
        ReturnNull());
    return currentBlock.AddStatements(new StatementSyntax[] {
        newConditional });
}
```

▓ **Note** Even though the rule is defined to require a match, you are inverting the logic so the code returns null if the condition does not match.

When you run this code, you'll get the same code that we wrote by hand in Chapter 3. You can see the results of running this code in Listing 5-21.

Listing 5-21. Generated GreetingRules

```
public class GreetingRules
{
    public string Rule1(IGreetingProfile data)
    {
        if (data.Hour > 11)
            return null;
        if (data.Gender != 1)
            return null;
        return "Good Morning Mr." + data.LastName;
    }

    public string Rule2(IGreetingProfile data)
    {
        if (data.Hour > 11)
            return null;
        if (data.Gender != 2)
            return null;
        if (data.MaritalStatus != 1)
            return null;
        return "Good Morning Mrs. " + data.LastName;
    }

    public string Rule3(IGreetingProfile data)
    {
        if (data.Hour > 11)
            return null;
        if (data.Gender != 2)
            return null;
        if (data.MaritalStatus != 2)
            return null;
        return "Good Morning Ms." + data.LastName;
    }
```

```
public string Rule4(IGreetingProfile data)
{
    if (data.Hour < 12)
        return null;
    if (data.Hour > 17)
        return null;
    if (data.Gender != 1)
        return null;
    return "Good Afternoon Mr. " + data.LastName;
}

public string Rule5(IGreetingProfile data)
{
    if (data.Hour < 12)
        return null;
    if (data.Hour > 17)
        return null;
    if (data.Gender != 2)
        return null;
    if (data.MaritalStatus != 1)
        return null;
    return "Good Afternoon Mrs. " + data.LastName;
}

public string Rule6(IGreetingProfile data)
{
    if (data.Hour < 12)
        return null;
    if (data.Hour > 17)
        return null;
    if (data.Gender != 2)
        return null;
    if (data.MaritalStatus != 2)
        return null;
    return "Good Afternoon Ms. " + data.LastName;
}
```

Automated Underwriting

As you saw in Chapter 3, underwriting rules require more than one table for their definition. This section explores an implementation that can define underwriting rules in two tables—UnderwritingRule and UnderwritingRuleDetail. There will be one record in the UnderwritingRule table for every UnderwritingRule and every record in the UnderwritingRuleDetail table with the same UnderwritingRuleId will be part of the definition for that underwriting rule.

▓ **Note**   Underwriting rule definitions are complicated by having their definitions spread over multiple tables and multiple records in the detail table.

You can gather all the relevant details to define the underwriting rules with two SQL queries, as shown in Listing 5-22.

Listing 5-22. Queries to Get the Underwriting Rule Metadata

```
SELECT  RuleName ,
        ShortDescription ,
        EffectiveDate ,
        ExpirationDate ,
        UnderwritingRuleId
FROM    dbo.UnderwritingRule;
```

And

```
SELECT  UnderwritingRuleDetailId ,
        UnderwritingRuleDetail.UnderwritingRuleId ,
        UnderwritingRuleDetail.LoanCodeId ,
        [Min] ,
        [Max] ,
        Sequence ,
        LoanCode.LoanCodeTypeId ,
        LoanCode.ShortDescription ,
        LoanCode.LongDescription,
                IsRange
FROM    dbo.UnderwritingRuleDetail
        INNER JOIN dbo.LoanCode ON LoanCode.LoanCodeId = UnderwritingRuleDetail.LoanCodeId
INNER JOIN dbo.LoanCodeType ON LoanCodeType.LoanCodeTypeId = LoanCode.LoanCodeTypeId
WHERE   UnderwritingRuleId = @RuleId
ORDER BY Sequence;
```

You can host these details in code using a couple of simple objects, as shown in Listing 5-23.

Listing 5-23. Containing Objects for Hosting the Underwriting Rule Metadata

```
public class UnderwritingRule
{
    public string RuleName { get; set; }
    public string ShortDescription { get; set; }
    public DateTime? EffectiveDate { get; set; }
    public DateTime? ExpirationDate { get; set; }
    public List<UnderwritingRuleDetail> Details { get; set; }
}
```

And

```
public class UnderwritingRuleDetail
{
    public int UnderwritingRuleDetailId { get; set; }
    public int UnderwritingRuleId { get; set; }
    public int LoanCodeId { get; set; }
    public decimal? Min { get; set; }
    public decimal? Max { get; set; }
```

```
    public int Sequence { get; set; }
    public int LoanCodeTypeId { get; set; }
    public string ShortDescription { get; set; }
    public string LongDescription { get; set; }
    public bool IsRange {get;set;}
}
```

When implementing the rules, we will add a slight change from Chapter 3. Instead of having a compound conditional listing each valid value for a given loan code, we will load the valid values in an array and see if the array of valid values contains the loan code value that was passed in. This inverts the logic a bit from what you might expect from looking at the raw data, but it makes the generated conditionals less complex. With this implementation, a complex conditional such as the one shown in Listing 5-24 can be converted to a more streamlined implementation, shown in Listing 5-25.

Listing 5-24. Direct Implementation of Evaluating Valid Values

```
private bool DirectLogic (ILoanCodes data)
{
    if (data.Code4 == 1 || data.Code4 == 2 || data.Code4 == 3 || data.Code5 == 4)
        return true;
    return false;
}
```

Listing 5-25. Reworking the Logic to Reduce Complexity

```
private bool ContainsLogic (ILoanCodes data)
{
    var target = new[] { 1, 2, 3, 4 };
    if (!target.Contains(data.Code4))
        return false;
    return true;
}
```

▦ **Note** Regardless of the number of valid values for any given loan code, the complexity of evaluating each condition will remain constant.

▦ **Tip** Any time you can reduce the complexity of the code to be generated, you are also reducing the complexity of the generator, which will reduce the chances that there are bugs in the generator.

The basic driving logic for generating these rules follows basic patterns that you have already seen, with a couple of twists. You start with a simple SyntaxTree for the class and a simple SyntaxTree for the method. Again, you implement each underwriting rule in its own method in the generated class, and each method will take a known interface, exposing all the data needed to evaluate these rules. The basic generator is shown in Listing 5-26.

Listing 5-26. Main Driver for Generating Underwriting Rules

```
public static void GenerateRules()
{
    var code = @"public class UnderwritingRules{}";
    var method = @"public bool Rule(ILoanCodes data)
        {
            var target = new []{};
        }";
    var syntaxTree = CSharpSyntaxTree.ParseText(code).GetRoot();
    var classDeclaration = syntaxTree.DescendantNodes()
        .OfType<ClassDeclarationSyntax>().FirstOrDefault();
    var originalDeclaration = classDeclaration;
    foreach (var rule in GetUnderwritingRules())
    {
        var methodSyntaxTree =
            CSharpSyntaxTree.ParseText(method).GetRoot();
        var underwritingRule = methodSyntaxTree.DescendantNodes()
            .OfType<MethodDeclarationSyntax>().FirstOrDefault();
        underwritingRule = RenameRule(rule.RuleName, underwritingRule);
        underwritingRule = underwritingRule
            .WithLeadingTrivia(new SyntaxTrivia[] {
            SyntaxFactory.Comment("// " + rule.ShortDescription) });
        underwritingRule = underwritingRule
            .WithBody( ProcessLoanCodes(rule, underwritingRule.Body));
        var currentBlock = underwritingRule.Body;
        currentBlock = currentBlock
            .AddStatements(new StatementSyntax[] { ReturnTrue() });
        underwritingRule = underwritingRule.WithBody(currentBlock);
        classDeclaration = classDeclaration
            .AddMembers(underwritingRule);
    }
    Console.WriteLine(classDeclaration.NormalizeWhitespace());
}
```

Most of the work to implement the rule is handled by the `ProcessLoanCodes` method. You have two types of processing that you need to deal with. The more common is where the actual value must match one of a list of valid values, such as `LoanPurpose` must be Refi Cash Out or Refi Debt Consolidation. The other scenario is where the `LoanCodeType` is a range and the actual value must be between the min and the max specified, such as LTV must be between 80% and 85%.

▓ **Note**   For the range-based rules, either the min or the max must be specified. Either one, or both, can be specified. The rule would not make sense and is probably not properly defined if both are left blank.

Regardless of the type of `LoanCode` you are dealing with, you start by grouping on the `LoanCodeType`. When there is more than one detail record for a given `LoanCodeType`, each detail record will define a valid value for that `LoanCode`. There will generally only be a single detail record when the `LoanCodeType` is a range, but having more than one record is valid and should be accommodated. Listing 5-27 shows how to deal with and accommodate these two types of loan codes.

Listing 5-27. Process LoanCodes

```
private static BlockSyntax ProcessLoanCodes(UnderwritingRule rule,
    BlockSyntax underwritingRule)
{
    var loanCodeTypes = from d in rule.Details
                        group d by new { d.LoanCodeTypeId, d.IsRange }
                        into loanCodes
                        select loanCodes;
    foreach (var loanCodeType in loanCodeTypes)
    {
        var loanCodeTypeId = loanCodeType.Key.LoanCodeTypeId;
        if (!loanCodeType.Key.IsRange)
        {
            var initializationExpressions = new
                List<LiteralExpressionSyntax>();
            foreach (var detail in loanCodeType)
            {
                initializationExpressions
                  .Add(SyntaxFactory.LiteralExpression
                    (SyntaxKind.StringLiteralExpression,
                     SyntaxFactory.Literal(detail.LoanCodeId)));
            }
            underwritingRule = ProcessLoanCodeCondition(loanCodeTypeId,
                underwritingRule, initializationExpressions);
        }
        else
        {
            foreach (var detail in loanCodeType)
            {
                if (detail.Max.HasValue)
                    underwritingRule = ProcessLoanCodeRangeCondition
                      (loanCodeTypeId, underwritingRule,
                        SyntaxKind.GreaterThanExpression,
                        detail.Max.Value);
                if (detail.Min.HasValue)
                    underwritingRule = ProcessLoanCodeRangeCondition
                      (loanCodeTypeId, underwritingRule,
                        SyntaxKind.LessThanExpression,
                        detail.Min.Value);
            }
        }
    }
    return underwritingRule;
}
```

▓ **Note**   underwritingRule gets tracked through the return value from these method calls because the SyntaxTree is immutable. The original tree never changes, so you have to keep replacing the reference to it with the latest version created every time a change is made.

ProcessLoanCodeCondition, as shown in Listing 5-28, is responsible for building up the target array and ensuring that the actual value passed in is in this list of valid values. Otherwise, it returns false.

Listing 5-28. ProcessLoanCodeCondition

```
private static BlockSyntax ProcessLoanCodeCondition(int loanCode,
    BlockSyntax currentBlock, List<LiteralExpressionSyntax> initializationExpressions)
{
    var assignmentStatement = ReinitializeTargetArray(currentBlock,
        initializationExpressions);

    currentBlock = currentBlock.AddStatements
        (new StatementSyntax[] { assignmentStatement });
    var codeExpression = SyntaxFactory.MemberAccessExpression(
            SyntaxKind.SimpleMemberAccessExpression,
            SyntaxFactory.IdentifierName("data"),
            SyntaxFactory.IdentifierName("Code" + loanCode));
    var target = SyntaxFactory.MemberAccessExpression
            (SyntaxKind.SimpleMemberAccessExpression,
                SyntaxFactory.IdentifierName("target"),
                SyntaxFactory.IdentifierName("Contains"));
    var argument = SyntaxFactory.Argument(codeExpression);
    var argumentList = SyntaxFactory.SeparatedList(new[] { argument });

    var contains = SyntaxFactory.InvocationExpression(target,
        SyntaxFactory.ArgumentList(argumentList));
    var notContains = SyntaxFactory.BinaryExpression
            (SyntaxKind.NotEqualsExpression, contains,
            SyntaxFactory.LiteralExpression
                (SyntaxKind.TrueLiteralExpression));
    var newConditional = SyntaxFactory.IfStatement(notContains,
        ReturnFalse());
    return currentBlock.AddStatements(new StatementSyntax[] {
        newConditional });
}
```

ReinitializeTargetArray will handle the logic for resetting the local variable "target" with the valid code values for the new code type. This logic is shown in Listing 5-29.

Listing 5-29. ReinitializeTargetArray

```
private static ExpressionStatementSyntax ReinitializeTargetArray
    (BlockSyntax currentBlock,
     List<LiteralExpressionSyntax> initializationExpressions)
{
    var declarator = currentBlock.DescendantNodes()
        .OfType<VariableDeclaratorSyntax>()
        .FirstOrDefault();
    var init = declarator.Initializer;
    var initializationExpression = currentBlock.DescendantNodes()
        .OfType<ImplicitArrayCreationExpressionSyntax>()
        .FirstOrDefault();
```

```
    initializationExpression = initializationExpression
        .AddInitializerExpressions
          (initializationExpressions.ToArray());
    var variableIdentifier = SyntaxFactory.IdentifierName("target");
    var assignment = SyntaxFactory.AssignmentExpression
          (SyntaxKind.SimpleAssignmentExpression,
           variableIdentifier, initializationExpression);
    var assignmentStatement =
          SyntaxFactory.ExpressionStatement(assignment);
    return assignmentStatement;
}
```

The logic for evaluating the range conditions is simpler and can leverage the same generation logic by simply changing the type of comparison being made, as shown in Listing 5-30.

Listing 5-30. ProcessLoanCodeRangeCondition

```
private static BlockSyntax ProcessLoanCodeRangeCondition
      (int loanCodeTypeId, BlockSyntax underwritingRule,
       SyntaxKind comparisonType, decimal codeValue)
{
    var codeExpression = SyntaxFactory.MemberAccessExpression(
          SyntaxKind.SimpleMemberAccessExpression,
          SyntaxFactory.IdentifierName("data"),
          SyntaxFactory.IdentifierName("Code" + loanCodeTypeId));
    var condition = SyntaxFactory.BinaryExpression(comparisonType,
        codeExpression,SyntaxFactory.LiteralExpression
          (SyntaxKind.NumericLiteralExpression,
           SyntaxFactory.Literal(codeValue)));
    var newConditional = SyntaxFactory.IfStatement(condition,
        ReturnFalse());
    return underwritingRule.AddStatements(new StatementSyntax[]
        { newConditional });
}
```

If you run the generator against the three underwriting rules from Chapter 3, you'll get the implementation shown in Listing 5-31.

Listing 5-31. Generated Underwriting Rules

```
public class UnderwritingRules
{
    // Full Doc requires 2 years Bank Statements for Purchase of Single Family Residence
    public bool FullDocRequirements(ILoanCodes data)
    {
        var target = new int [] { };
        target = new[] { 1 };
        if (target.Contains(data.Code1) != true)
            return false;
        target = new[] { 7 };
```

```
        if (target.Contains(data.Code3) != true)
            return false;
        target = new[] { 10, 11 };
        if (target.Contains(data.Code4) != true)
            return false;
        target = new[] { 4, 5, 6 };
        if (target.Contains(data.Code2) != true)
            return false;
        return true;
    }

    // Appraisal with 3 Comps required for Purchase
    public bool AppraisalRequirements(ILoanCodes data)
    {
        var target = new int [] { };
        target = new[] { 7 };
        if (target.Contains(data.Code3) != true)
            return false;
        target = new[] { 21 };
        if (target.Contains(data.Code6) != true)
            return false;
        target = new[] { 16, 17, 18 };
        if (target.Contains(data.Code5) != true)
            return false;
        return true;
    }

    // Maximum LTV is 80% if the Credit Score is below 650 on a Refinance unless the DTI is
    below 40%
    public bool LTVGuideline(ILoanCodes data)
    {
        var target = new int[] { };
        target = new[] { 8, 9 };
        if (target.Contains(data.Code3) != true)
            return false;
        if (data.Code10 > 650M)
            return false;
        if (data.Code8 > 40M)
            return false;
        if (data.Code9 > 80M)
            return false;
        return true;
    }
}
```

▓ **Note**   The M at the end of numeric literal instructs the compiler that the value should be treated as a decimal. You may also find the suffixes L, D, F, and U. These represent Long, Double, Float, and Unsigned, respectively. This is one of the few cases where C# is not case sensitive. You can use m, l, d, or u as well, but typical conventions stick to the uppercase.

Summary

Throughout this book, we have focused on a couple of recurring types of business logic that should help to highlight a broader range of possible business scenarios. While we have focused a lot of attention on the Hello World greeting rules and the generalized underwriting rules, the concepts and best practices followed here apply to many different scenarios. Some of these best practices include:

- Define a separate simple class to house the metadata driving your code generation.

- Separate retrieving and mapping the metadata from the code-generation process.

- Simplify the logic for the code to be generated anytime you can. This will simplify the code generator, which will improve the quality of the generated code.

- Always remember that Roslyn objects are immutable. Return values from method calls must be saved and incorporated back into the original SyntaxTree or the changes will be lost.

Now that you have explored how to structure data to express business logic and how to use Roslyn to generate business logic, you are ready to turn your attention to how to deploy this generated code.

CHAPTER 6

Deploying Generated Code

So far, we have simply written the generated code to the screen, but this is hardly the only option. Remember Roslyn is the compiler. When you have a generated SyntaxTree, you are already partway through compilation.

To facilitate taking the process from SyntaxTree to compiled assembly, we will start with a simple solution preloaded with the needed references and an empty project. Only code that you generate will be in this project.

Note   Supporting code like the interfaces used as parameters should be defined in a separate assembly, accessed by both the generated code and the code using the generated code.

Setting Up the Sample Solution

Start by creating a new solution. In this solution, you will need two projects, one we will call EmptyProject and the other called CommonProject. The EmptyProject will be just that, empty. This project should only contain code that is generated. The CommonProject will contain the various interfaces used by the generated code. This is the common project because it will be referenced by both the generated code in the empty project, as well as any project that will call the methods in the generated code. So, EmptyProject will need a reference to CommonProject, as shown in Figure 6-1.

Tip   We want to keep these two projects in a separate solution because the code that you will run will manipulate EmptyProject, which will complicate debugging if it is not in a separate solution.

© Nick Harrison 2017

N. Harrison, *Code Generation with Roslyn*, DOI 10.1007/978-1-4842-2211-9_6

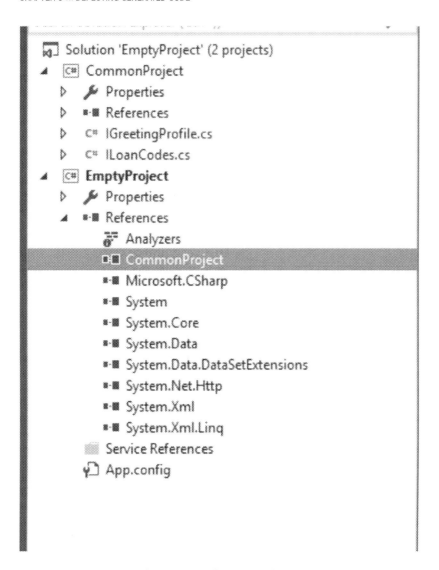

Figure 6-1. Project setup for compiling the generated code

The Basic Flow

The build process is straightforward:

1. Load the sample solution into a workspace.

2. Find the empty project in that solution.

3. Add the resulting SyntaxTree for the generated code to the project.

4. Set the compilation options.

5. Get the compilation.

6.   Review any diagnostic messages.

7.   Emit the compiled assembly.

Sounds simple enough, but there are some details to be worked through. Once you work through these details, this process can be used to compile any generated code.

You can express the flow for compiling generated code as shown in Listing 6-1.

Listing 6-1. Basic Flow for Compiling Generated Code

```
public static void CompileUnderwritingRules()
{
    var work = MSBuildWorkspace.Create();
    var project = LoadEmptyProject(work);
    var generator = new UnderwritingRuleGenerator();
    var tree = generator.GenerateRules();
    var doc = SafeAddDocument(project, tree, "UnderwritingRules");
    if (!work.TryApplyChanges(doc.Project.Solution))
        Console.WriteLine
                ("Failed to add the generated code to the project");
    project = doc.Project;
    project = AddCompilationOptions(project);
    var compiler = project.GetCompilationAsync().Result;
    if (ReviewDiagnosticMessages(compiler))
        compiler.Emit("UnderwritingRules.dll");
}
```

Loading the EmptyProject

Let's look at these individual pieces one at a time, starting with loading the empty project, as shown in Listing 6-2.

Listing 6-2. Loading the Empty Project

```
private static Project LoadEmptyProject( MSBuildWorkspace work)
{
    var solution = work.OpenSolutionAsync(PATH_TO_SOLUTION).Result;
    var project = solution.Projects.FirstOrDefault
            (p => p.Name == "EmptyProject");
    if (project == null)
        throw new Exception("Could not find the empty project");
    return project;
}
```

This method will be standard across most code generation approaches. The only thing likely to change is the name of the project you want to add your code to—not everyone will want to call it `EmptyProject`— and the path to the solution where this project is located. You may want to even pull this value from a configuration file.

░ **Note**   The `UnderwritingRuleGenerator` with the `GenerateRules` method is the same object developed in Chapter 5. You will make some changes to it shortly.

Safely Add a New Document

SafeAddDocument has a couple of subtle nuances that you need to be aware of. We call it SafeAddDocument because it can safely handle the scenario in which the document being added is already in the project. Without this safety net in place, the same document will be added to the project, which will cause errors when you try to compile the project. Listing 6-3 shows the full implementation of SafeAddDocument.

▨ **Caution**   You will not get an error when you add the document multiple times; you will get an error when you try to compile that can be confusing. It will also look strange when the same file is listed multiple times in Solution Explorer. You will get an error about the file being specified more than once by the Sources parameter.

Listing 6-3. Safely Adding a New Document to a Project

```
private static Document SafeAddDocument( Project project,
    SyntaxTree tree, string documentName)
{
    var targetDocument = project.Documents
        .FirstOrDefault(d => d.Name.StartsWith(documentName));
    if (targetDocument != null)
    {
        project = project.RemoveDocument(targetDocument.Id);
    }
    var doc = project.AddDocument(documentName, tree.GetRoot()
        .NormalizeWhitespace());
    return doc;
}
```

You can start by searching for a document matching the name that you are looking for. If you find one, explicitly remove it. Then you can safely add the document. Once the document has been added to the project, you must use the workspace to apply the changes to the project. Remember that Roslyn objects are immutable.

Specifying Compilation Options

With Roslyn, you can specify every compiler option you want. Listing 6-4 shows how to add options to specify a release build for a DLL running on any CPU.

Listing 6-4. Adding the Compilation Options

```
private static Project AddCompilationOptions(Project project)
{
    var options = new CSharpCompilationOptions(
            OutputKind.DynamicallyLinkedLibrary)
                .WithOptimizationLevel(OptimizationLevel.Release)
                .WithPlatform(Platform.AnyCpu)
                .WithModuleName("GeneratedCode");
    project = project.WithCompilationOptions(options);
    return project;
}
```

This will cover most scenarios you are likely to encounter for generating business logic, but the Roslyn libraries are complete with support for every potential scenario. `CSharpCompilationOptions` has methods to support such obscure scenarios as:

- Allowing unsafe code

- Concurrent builds

- Options for signing the assembly

- Disabling overflow checks

Once the compiler options are specified, you are ready to get the compilation results. This is potentially a long running method so it is set up to be run asynchronously, but you don't really have anything else to run while you are waiting on the method to finish. You can make it run synchronously by immediately accessing the `Result` property of the resulting task:

```
var compiler = project.GetCompilationAsync().Result;
```

▓ **Note** You can convert an asynchronous process into a synchronous process by immediately accessing the `Result` property of the task that was returned. The `get` accessor for this property ensures that the task is complete before returning.

Reviewing the Diagnostic Messages

The result is a compilation that you can use to review any diagnostic messages as well as output the resulting assembly if there were no errors. Listing 6-5 shows a generalized process for reviewing error messages.

Listing 6-5. Reviewing the Diagnostic Messages from the Compiler

```
private static bool ReviewDiagnosticMessages(Compilation compiler)
{
    var results = compiler.GetDiagnostics();
    var returnValue = true;
    foreach (var item in results.Where(i => i.Severity == DiagnosticSeverity.Error))
    {
        returnValue = false;
        Console.WriteLine(item.GetMessage() + item.Location);
    }
    return returnValue;
}
```

If there are no errors, you can successfully emit an assembly. If there are errors, it shows the diagnostic message as well as the details for the code that caused the problems.

▓ **Tip** Depending on your standards, you may want to be stricter and require that all warnings be resolved as well. If so, simply change the conditional in the `Where` clause that feeds the `foreach`.

Using the code generator from Chapter 5, you will get some error messages. This is not surprising. Code rarely compiles the first time (see Listing 6-6).

Listing 6-6. Original Compiler Error Messages

```
The type or namespace name 'ILoanCodes' could not be found (are you missing a using
directive or an assembly reference?)
        SourceFile(UnderwritingRules[161..171))
The type or namespace name 'ILoanCodes' could not be found (are you missing a using
directive or an assembly reference?)
        SourceFile(UnderwritingRules[783..793))
The type or namespace name 'ILoanCodes' could not be found (are you missing a using
directive or an assembly reference?)
        SourceFile(UnderwritingRules[1337..1347))
'int[]' does not contain a definition for 'Contains' and no extension method 'Contains'
accepting a first argument of type 'int[]' could be found (are you missing a using directive
or an assembly reference?)
        SourceFile(UnderwritingRules[268..276))
'int[]' does not contain a definition for 'Contains' and no extension method 'Contains'
accepting a first argument of type 'int[]' could be found (are you missing a using directive
or an assembly reference?)
        SourceFile(UnderwritingRules[376..384))
```

■ **Note**   You can also see these same messages by manually adding the generated code to an existing project and explicitly compiling it. The compiler providing the error messages is the same regardless of whether you are using Visual Studio or Roslyn directly.

The full error messages have been truncated for brevity. It is common to see the same error message repeated dozens or hundreds of times. Don't let this overwhelm you. In this case, there are only two problems. You need to add a couple of using statements to the beginning of the class declaration.

You can resolve these compiler errors by changing the GenerateRules method in UnderwritingRuleGenerator to reflect the changes shown in Listing 6-7.

Listing 6-7. Revised GenerateRules

```
public SyntaxTree GenerateRules()
  {
      var code = @"using CommonProject;
                  using System.Linq;
                  public class UnderwritingRules{}";
      var method = @"public bool Rule(ILoanCodes data)
          {
              var target = new []{0};
          }";
      var syntaxTree = CSharpSyntaxTree.ParseText(code).GetRoot();
      var classDeclaration =
          syntaxTree.DescendantNodes().OfType<ClassDeclarationSyntax>()
          .FirstOrDefault();
      var originalClass = classDeclaration;
      foreach (var rule in GetUnderwritingRules())
```

```
    {
        var methodSyntaxTree =
            CSharpSyntaxTree.ParseText(method).GetRoot();
        var underwritingRule = methodSyntaxTree.DescendantNodes()
            .OfType<MethodDeclarationSyntax>().FirstOrDefault();
        underwritingRule = RenameRule(rule.RuleName, underwritingRule);
        underwritingRule = underwritingRule
            .WithLeadingTrivia(new SyntaxTrivia[] {
                SyntaxFactory.Comment("// " + rule.ShortDescription) });
        underwritingRule =
                underwritingRule.WithBody(ProcessLoanCodes(rule,
                    underwritingRule.Body));
        var currentBlock = underwritingRule.Body;
        currentBlock = currentBlock.AddStatements(new StatementSyntax[]
                { ReturnTrue() });
        underwritingRule = underwritingRule.WithBody(currentBlock);
        classDeclaration =
            classDeclaration.AddMembers(underwritingRule);
    }
    var newNode = syntaxTree.ReplaceNode(originalClass,
        classDeclaration);
    return newNode.SyntaxTree;
}
```

Emitting an Assembly

With these code changes in place, you can run the compiler and this time you won't see any error messages. With no error messages reported, you can emit the assembly from the compiler (see Listing 6-8).

Listing 6-8. Emitting an Assembly

```
if (ReviewDiagnosticMessages(compiler))
    compiler.Emit("UnderwritingRules.dll");
```

Emitting an assembly to a file is not the only option, but it will be the one that we will follow most often. You could also emit it to a stream, as shown in Listing 6-9.

Listing 6-9. Emitting to a Memory Stream

```
private static Assembly EmitMemoryStream(Compilation compiler)
{
    using (var ms = new MemoryStream())
    {
        compiler.Emit(ms);
        ms.Seek(0, SeekOrigin.Begin);
        return Assembly.Load(ms.ToArray());
    }
}
```

This can be helpful if you plan to generate the assembly and immediately run it without preserving it to disk. This may be appropriate in some situations where the generated code is extremely volatile or when the overhead of tracking when to regenerate the assembly is cumbersome.

▓ **Tip**   In most cases, you will regenerate the business logic on a set schedule and redeploy a new assembly as part of that schedule. That way, you don't incur the overhead of regenerating the code outside of this schedule.

Summary

In this chapter, you saw a general approach for taking generated code and producing an assembly. This process is the same regardless of the type of business logic you are working with. The basic flow is the same and in individual scenarios, you will have minimal changes to accommodate your specific configuration.

Deployment is just a simple matter of copying the resulting assembly to where ever it is needed. Creating the assembly is the same regardless of the business logic and how it will be used, but using the assembly may very well depend on the business logic that was created. In Chapter 7, we turn our attention to using the assembly to call the business logic that we generated.

CHAPTER 7

Reflecting on Generated Code

Generated code will always be code that was not known at compile time. The whole point of generating code is to make it easier to change the business rules after deployment. This is where *reflection* comes in. Reflection allows you to access metadata about your code at runtime. With it, you can load an assembly, discover the types in the assembly, create an instance of these types, and systematically execute any method discovered in these types. This is exactly what you need to evaluate new business logic.

Reflection may seem like magic, but it really is a matter of carefully applying a handful of useful programming tricks to build useful processing logic.

Loading the Assembly

Before you can do anything with reflection, you need to load the assembly you want to reflect on. This may seem like a trivial task, but there are some subtle issues to consider. The assembly object exposes static methods for loading an assembly. When you have several options, it is not always clear which is the best choice:

- Load with an AssemblyName
- Load with a Byte [ ]
- Load with a string
- Use LoadFile
- Use LoadFrom

Note   Each of these methods also provides overloads for specifying evidence, but these overloads are obsolete as of .NET Framework Version 4 and should be avoided.

The AssemblyName overload allows you to specify the simple name, version, culture, and cryptographic key associated with the assembly. This allows you be very explicit about the assembly you want without having to give the actual path to the assembly. This may be useful in many cases, but for these purposes, you have complete control over the path so that is not an issue.

The load with a Byte [] option is like what you saw at the end of Chapter 6, where you loaded an assembly from a memory stream emitted from the compiler. In this case, you would read the assembly directly from the file into a Byte [] and pass that Byte [] to the Load method. This has the advantage of not locking the file on disk that contains the assembly.

© Nick Harrison 2017
N. Harrison, *Code Generation with Roslyn*, DOI 10.1007/978-1-4842-2211-9_7

> ▓ **Note**   This method will work only if the project loading the assembly and executing methods in the types has a reference to `CommonProject`, referenced in Chapter 7.

`LoadFile` and `LoadFrom` are very similar with subtle differences that can lead to confusion. For these purposes, you may never notice the differences, but they are still important. The most fundamental difference revolves around how dependencies are resolved. `LoadFile` will load only the Assembly specified. If there are any dependencies, they will not be handled by the internal dependency resolution logic. `LoadFrom` uses the internal dependency resolution logic and will automatically attempt to load any dependent assemblies for you. Also, `LoadFrom` may not load the expected version. If a different version with the same identity is already loaded, the previously loaded version must be used.

> ▓ **Note**   There are a lot of subtle nuances involved in loading assemblies. You may have issues with the context, resolving dependencies, loading multiple versions, etc. You can bypass many of these nuances based on the limited scope because you are using the loaded assembly and the fact that you can tightly control the dependencies in the generated assembly.

The remaining code in this chapter is based on loading the assembly from a `Byte []`. If you are using a dependency injection framework or already have a preferred method for loading assemblies, the rest of the examples dealing with reflection work regardless of how you loaded the assembly.

Loading by a `Byte []` has the following advantages:

- The original file will not be locked and can be overridden without affecting the running application.

- The load process doesn't incur the overhead of probing for an assembly like the various other methods do.

- We can potentially load multiple versions at the same time. This can be useful if you have different assemblies implementing different date-specific business logic.

- We don't have to worry about assembly probing redirecting us to a different version. We get the exact bits from the location that we read from to get the `Byte []`.

Listing 7-1 shows a very simple implementation of loading by `Byte []`. Key error handling has been omitted for the sake of simplicity.

Listing 7-1. Loading an Assembly from a Byte []

```
public Assembly LoadByteArray()
{
    var source = File.ReadAllBytes(PathToAssembly);
    var assembly = Assembly.Load(source);
    return assembly;
}
```

Monitoring for Changes

Because you loaded the assembly from a `Byte []` in this example, you don't have the underlying file locked. This file can be replaced with updated logic at any time. This means that you need to be able to detect that the file has changed and refresh the loaded assembly as needed.

> ▓ **Tip**   Because loading an assembly is an expensive operation, you don't want to reload every time you reference it. To improve performance and still be responsive to changes, you can check the file when you reference the assembly and reload it only if the file has changed.

Listing 7-2 shows an updated LoadByteArray method using caching to return a new assembly only if the underlying file has changed since the last time the assembly was loaded.

Listing 7-2. Loading an Assembly with Caching

```
public Assembly LoadByteArray()
{
    var file = new FileInfo(PathToAssembly);
    if (localAssembly == null)
    {
        InternalLoadAssembly(file);
    }
    if (file.LastWriteTimeUtc > lastModificationDate)
    {
        InternalLoadAssembly(file);
    }
    return localAssembly;
}

private void InternalLoadAssembly(FileInfo file)
{
    var source = File.ReadAllBytes(file.FullName);
    localAssembly = Assembly.Load(source);
    lastModificationDate = file.LastWriteTimeUtc;
}
```

With this caching in place, we will get the latest copy of the assembly every time we request the assembly without having to incur the overhead of reloading it every time.

Discovering Types

Generally, each type would have methods for a single type of rule. For example, you might have a type for general underwriting rules with separate types for Max LTV Rules and Max Loan Amount Rules, or you might have separate types for each loan program offered. You could have a type for the qualifying rules for coverage type in an insurance policy management system. You could have a type for the various greetings in CMS, or a type for the rules to determine shipping costs and promotions for an e-commerce site. Any number of business rules can be embedded in generated assemblies.

Once you have an assembly, you have two methods to use to get the types in that assembly—GetType and GetTypes. If you know that you are only interested in a single type, the GetType() method is the one to use. If you are interested in multiple types, call the GetTypes() method and search the returning list of types for the ones you want.

░ **Tip**   If you need a single type, explicitly get it with `GetType()`. If you need several types, call `GetTypes()` and then search for the ones you want against the returned array of types.

░ **Caution**   Calling `GetTypes()` is not without risk. If any type cannot be loaded, the entire call will fail and throw the exception `ReflectionTypeLoadException` and you will not get any data.

Listing 7-3 shows how to explicitly search by name to find `UnderwritingRules`. Here, we specify not to throw an exception if the type is not found. Instead, the method will return a null value that you can deal with more explicitly. We also specify not to ignore case in doing the search. Doing a case-insensitive search would slow the search down and is not necessary because we should all be aware that C# is case sensitive.

Listing 7-3. Finding the UnderwritingRules Class

```
private static Type GetUnderwritingRules (Assembly assembly)
{
    var throwOnError = false;
    var ignoreCase = false;
    var type = assembly.GetType("UnderwritingRules", throwOnError, ignoreCase);
    return type;
}
```

If you need multiple types, you can retrieve them all with a single call to `GetTypes()` and then filter the results, as shown in Listing 7-4.

Listing 7-4. Getting Multiple Types Based on Their Name

```
private static IEnumerable<Type> GetFullUnderwritingRules(Assembly assembly)
{
    var targetTypes = new[] { "UnderwritingRules", "MaxLTV", "MaxLoanAmount", "Fixed",
    "ARM" };
    var types = assembly.GetTypes().Where(t => targetTypes.Contains(t.FullName));
    return types;
}
```

Once we have a `Type` object, the name is not the only value you can filter by. You can modify the Code Generator to add a custom attribute that could then be used to filter against. Suppose that all the generated rules are in classes that have an `UnderwritingRuleAttribute` added to the class declaration. Regardless of how many types are involved, you'll get them all with the code shown in Listing 7-5.

Listing 7-5. Getting Types Based on an Attribute

```
private static IEnumerable<Type> GetFullUnderwritingRulesByAttribute(Assembly assembly)
{
    var types = assembly.GetTypes().Where
        (t => t.GetCustomAttribute<UnderwritingRuleAttribute>() != null);
    return types;
}
```

You could also identify the underwriting rules by base class. Suppose that all your generated rules are in classes derived from BaseUnderwritingRule. You can get them all with the code shown in Listing 7-6.

Listing 7-6. Getting Types Based on a Base Class

```
private static IEnumerable<Type> GetFullUnderwritingRulesByBaseClass (Assembly assembly)
{
    var types = assembly.GetTypes().Where
        (t => t.IsSubclassOf(typeof(BaseUnderwritingClass)));
    return types;
}
```

Discovering Methods

Regardless of how you find the types defining the business rules, you can loop through these types to find the methods implementing the business rules. In general, this will be every method defined in the class, but you can put a few safety checks in place to ensure that you don't run unintended code. For example, say you want to make sure to only get the methods defined at this level of inheritance and not inherited from a base class, as shown in Listing 7-7.

Listing 7-7. Finding the Public Methods at this Level of Inheritance

```
private IEnumerable<MethodInfo> GetBusinessRules (Type rule)
{
    var rules = rule.GetMethods(BindingFlags.DeclaredOnly
        | BindingFlags.Instance
        | BindingFlags.Public);
    return rules;
}
```

This code will filter out methods like ToString, GetHashCode, etc. that are automatically inherited from System.Object, but there could still be methods included that are not actual business rules. As a further restriction, you can filter down to include only the methods that match the expected signature. In the case of the UnderwritingRules generated in Chapter 6, you were interested in methods returning a Boolean value and accepting an ILoanCodes parameter. Listing 7-8 shows how to implement such a filter.

Listing 7-8. Filtering the Methods Based on Return Type and Parameters

```
private IEnumerable<MethodInfo> GetFilteredBusinessRules(Type rule)
{
    var rules = rule.GetMethods(BindingFlags.DeclaredOnly
        | BindingFlags.Instance
        | BindingFlags.Public).Where(m=>m.ReturnType == typeof(bool)
        && m.GetParameters().Count() == 1
        && m.GetParameters().All(p=>p.ParameterType == typeof (ILoanCodes)));
    return rules;
}
```

Calling Methods

Once you have identified the methods that implement your business rules, you are ready to invoke them. You need two things to call these methods. Most importantly, you need an instance of an object implementing the ILoanCodes interface populated with the details for a loan. Secondly, you need an instance of the type defining the rules.

▓ **Tip**   You need an instance of the type containing the methods only because you did not define the methods as static. If you define the methods as static, you can skip this requirement.

The ILoanCodes object will generally be passed in from the UI or some other source, but it is also easy to mock because it is a simple object exposing a handful of read/write properties. For these purposes, we will mock this object with some hard-coded values like what you would do in unit testing. A simple object representing the ILoanCodes is shown in Listing 7-9.

When it comes to evaluating the rules, we don't really care where the data comes from. Initializing the ILoanCodes object is shown in Listing 7-10.

Listing 7-9. Implementing the ILoanCodes interface

```
public class StaticLoanCodes : ILoanCodes
{
        public int Code1 { get; set; }
        public int Code2 { get; set; }
        public int Code3 { get; set; }
        public int Code4 { get; set; }
        public int Code5 { get; set; }
        public int Code6 { get; set; }
        public int Code7 { get; set; }
        public decimal Code8 { get; set; }
        public decimal Code9 { get; set; }
        public decimal Code10 { get; set; }
}
```

Listing 7-10. Initializing the StaticLoanCodes

```
private ILoanCodes InitializeLoanCodes()
{
    return new StaticLoanCodes
    {
        Code1 = 1,  // Doc Type
        Code2 = 5,  // Number of months bank statements
        Code3 = 7,  // Loan Purpose
        Code4 = 10, // Property Type
        Code5 = 18, // Appraisal Type
        Code6 = 20, // Comps
        Code7 = 23, // Location
        Code8 = 44.87M, // DTI
        Code9 = 89.46M, // LTV
        Code10 = 668  // Credit Score
    };
}
```

Creating an instance of the type defining the rules is trivial with the `Activator` object, as shown in Listing 7-11. This code will call the default constructor for the type specified.

▓ **Caution**   If you don't have a default constructor—one with no parameters—you will get an error. The activator could throw a `MissingMethodException` if it cannot find the default constructor. You might also get a `TargetInvokationExpression` that wraps any exceptions thrown by the constructor.

Listing 7-11. Creating an Instance of the Rule

```
private static object CreateBusinessRule (Type rule)
{
    return Activator.CreateInstance(rule);
}
```

▓ **Tip**   You can skip this step if the methods implementing the rules are defined as `static`. For `static` methods, you can pass in `null` instead of an instance of the object.

With these pieces in place, you are ready to run each of the business rules, as shown in Listing 7-12.

Listing 7-12. Running the Underwriting Rules

```
private static IEnumerable<RuleResult> RunRules (Type rule)
{
    var instance = CreateBusinessRule(rule);
    var codes = InitializeLoanCodes();
    var methods = GetFilteredBusinessRules(rule);
    var results = new List<RuleResult>();
    foreach (var method in methods)
    {
        results.Add(new RuleResult
        {
            Result = (bool)method.Invoke(instance, new[] { codes }),
            RuleName = method.Name
        });
    }
    return results;
}
```

▓ **Caution**   A lot of logic has been stripped out to not distract from the main points. You will need to add appropriate error handling before this is ready for prime time.

In this example, you run each rule once, keeping track of which ones pass and which ones fail. Depending on your requirements, you may want to halt processing as soon as a single rule fails. You may also want to track more information than simply the name of the methods for reporting the results, but this shows the basic mechanics for running the rules.

Interpreting the Results

Now that you can run the rules and track the result for each rule, you are ready to interpret the results. This will be specific to your business requirements. In the simplest case, you may want to simply display to the users a message that all the rules passed or list the ones that did not pass. This interpretation is shown in Listing 7-13.

Listing 7-13. Simple Evaluation of the Business Rules

```
private static void EvaluateUnderwritingRules(Assembly assembly)
{
    var rules = GetFullUnderwritingRules(assembly);
    foreach (var rule in rules)
    {
        Console.Write(rule.FullName);
        var results = RunRules(rule);
        if (results.Any(r => r.Result == false))
        {
            Console.WriteLine(" the following rules failed:");
            foreach (var result in results.Where(r => r.Result == false))
            {
                Console.WriteLine("\t" + result.RuleName);
            }
        }
        else
            Console.WriteLine(" all rules Passed!");
    }
}
```

Based on the data used to initialize the StaticLoanCodes and the sample rules you've been working with, EvaluateUnderwritingRules produces the following output:

```
UnderwritingRules the following rules failed:
        AppraisalRequirements
        LTVGuideline
```

▒ **Note**   The code shown in Listings 7-12 and 7-13 can handle any number of rules, whether it is the small set of three sample rules we defined here or the thousands of rules you are likely to have in a real-world scenario. Just be sure to add the appropriate error handling and logging logic.

Depending on your business requirements, you want to halt processing as soon as you find one rule that passes or one rule that fails. You may define a higher-level grouping and determine that a grouping is valid if all the associated rules passed. These rules, combined with grouping rules, give you a great deal of flexibility for defining business logic for many different scenarios.

Summary

Reflection often has a bad reputation for being hard to understand or causing performance problems. This chapter discussed some guidelines to help minimize any performance issues and worked through the nuances for how to make this magic work.

You explored various approaches for loading assemblies.

You saw how to discover the types in a loaded assembly and explored various approaches for filtering down to the types that you are interested in. After you found the relevant types, you learned how to discover all the methods in these types.

You also learned various ways to filter through these methods and then execute the ones you're interested in.

Finally, you learned a couple of different ways to interpret the results from running these methods.

Armed with this knowledge, you are ready to apply these techniques to solve problems in your business applications.

CHAPTER 8

Best Practices

We have covered a lot of material in this book. Along the way, we touched on various best practices. Some were expressly called out as tips and notes. Others were stated but a bit more subtly. In this last chapter, we review these best practices as a handy reference.

Defining Requirements

Always Plan on Change

There are very few rules that will never change. Cutoff amounts will likely change. Dollar amounts for charges, prices, and fees will likely change, and qualification criteria will all change over time. Business moves too quickly to afford to spend much time adapting to these changes. Design applications to respond to changing requirements as quickly as possible.

Most Business Rules Are Date-Sensitive

You may not always be told about date sensitivity in advance, but you will often have to honor old requirements or logic. It might be honoring shipping costs when an order is placed versus when it ships, as these two dates are not always the same. It might be following underwriting guidelines based on origination date versus closing date or determining coverage limits based on proximity to hurricane season. Design to be able to rerun key transactions from different dates.

Structuring Logic

Separate Business Logic Tables from Business Entity Tables

This way you can potentially use the logic tables and supporting code in multiple lines of business applications as needed. Design data models so that the two models are self-contained and can have full constraints with no dependencies.

Integrate Lookup Tables into the Entity Data Model

This will allow you to explicitly define appropriate referential constraints to help improve data quality. Use lookup tables to specify valid values for key attributes. Add EffectiveDate and ExpirationDate columns to these tables to track how valid values change over time. Use strongly typed columns in the lookup tables so that the values entered can be properly tracked and any applicable constraints are enforced.

Avoid One True Lookup Tables (OTLT) in the Entity Data Model

An OTLT negates all the data integrity benefits that could be gained from using traditional lookup tables. It is difficult to track which code type goes with which foreign key, this complicates foreign key constraints. The data types and constraints for the value columns will be loose, meaning that you cannot properly constrain the values entered for the lookup items.

An OTLT Can Be Used to Simplify Expression-Based Decision Tables

The OTLT and the associated Rule Detail tables should be separated from the Entity Data Model, which will help mitigate the risk to data integrity that OTLT can introduce. Data in the logic tables, including the OTLT, are not used for transaction data. These tables are used to define and implement business rules and will not have any references back to transaction data. If there are references back to the transaction data, refer to the best practice "Separate Business Logic Tables from Business Entity Tables".

Types of Logic Tables

Type	Description
Simple lookup	A simple lookup table with additional data associated with each entry.
Decision table	Also known as a lookup table with multiple parameters. All of the parameters, some of which may be null, are used to select the appropriate record or records.
Compound decision table	Separates the rule definition from the rule details allowing you to have multiple variations on the rule definition. As long as any of the rule definitions apply, the rule applies. This allows you to have conditions that are joined as "or" requirements instead of only as "and" requirements.
Expression-based decision table	Similar to a compound decision table, but every transaction-level attribute that could be used is not explicitly defined, giving great flexibility for the rule definitions. Individual rule definition records may define specific operators to be used to evaluate the filters. This table structure is always evaluated in code.

Use Dates

Whether it is a simple lookup table, lookup table with multiple parameters, a decision table, compound decision table, or expression based decision table, add columns for Effective Date and Expiration Date to help support date-based business logic as well as honoring old business logic. If the record is always in effect, leave both dates null. If the record has not expired, leave the expiration date null. If the record was in effect since the beginning of the system, leave the effective date blank. Any query accessing data should compare the effective date and expiration date such as current date or to a known date from the transaction being processed. Only records active during the date specified should be returned. If either date field is null, it cannot be used to exclude a record from being returned.

Add Comment Columns to Logic Tables

Add columns for comments to every logic table you can. Encourage anyone maintaining the logic data to add comments to help explain the logic being defined. This will often be subject matter experts (SMEs) who will have substantial business knowledge to share in these comments. Such insights into the business logic could not easily be gathered any other way. These comments can be very valuable to help ensure that the logic being defined does what is intended by the business users.

Writing Code from Structured Logic

Hand-Write Sample Code Before Generating the Code

Hand-write the code that is implied by the logic table to ensure that the logic table provides all the data needed to create the code. Hand-writing the code also provides a template for what the generated code should look like. This will make it easier to generate the code as well as verify that the generate code fits the expected pattern.

Define an Input Interface

Define an interface with a read/write property with every transaction-level attribute needed to define the business rules being generated. This interface can be implemented from multiple sources without affecting how the rules work. You may use mock objects for testing, and then implement the interface directly by the UI or by separate objects defined in the business layer. The interface will have no dependencies with the true data model from the transaction system, which allows the same tools, tables, and code generators to work across multiple line of business applications.

Not All Logic Tables Should Be Converted to Code

If the logic can readily be interpreted through a query, keep it in the database. This is often true with lookup tables with multiple parameters. Let the database do what it does best and churn through the records, finding the ones that match the defining criteria.

   If the business logic for a single business transaction can be identified and interpreted with a single query, there is no benefit to pulling it over to code. If evaluating the business logic for a transaction requires multiple round trips to the database, pulling the business logic into code will improve processing time and take a load off of the database. The thresholds for how many round trips to the database are acceptable will vary depending on your application volume.

Generate Enums from Lookup Tables

Enums can and should be generated from lookup tables. Code written using enums will be easier to read and follow than code written using magic strings or magic numbers. Refactoring tools can update references to enum values that would be left unchanged if they were string literals or numeric literals. Magic strings and magic constants are string or numeric literals provided with no supporting context for the value.

   `if (gender ==1)` is much harder to follow than `if (gender == GenderType.Male)`

Incorporate Comments

Incorporate any comments that have been added to the logic tables you are basing your code on. This will help explain what the code does and help ensure that it solves the problem, or prevents the problem, that it was intended to solve. If you followed the earlier best practice, "Add Comment Columns to Logic Tables", the comments you incorporate into your code will add business value as well.

Fail Early

Business logic constructed with multiple conditional statements should have the most restrictive condition listed first to avoid extra processing time in scenarios that can readily be identified as irrelevant.

Using Roslyn

Roslyn Is the Compiler

Roslyn is a reimagining of the compiler. With it, you can interrupt the process to explore and interact with the immediate results. Roslyn is not an afterthought or external partially supported utility. When you compile code from Visual Studio, you are using the same libraries that you are using when you write a Roslyn-based utility. This means that Roslyn will always have full support of every language feature and structure that you can use or create when writing any application.

Roslyn Is Better for Code Generation

Roslyn is better for code generation than T4 because T4 cannot easily accommodate complex conditional logic common in business logic. T4, being template based, assumes that the code it creates will always follow a well-defined pattern. This is not the case when defining the subtle nuances of most business rules.

Roslyn is better for code generation than CodeDom because CodeDom does not support every language feature and has not kept pace as new language features such as LINQ and Lamda functions have been added. Roslyn can fully support every language feature available and faithfully reproduce any code fragment you could come up with.

Parse Sample Code

Roslyn allows you to start with a sample of what you want your code to look like and build from there. This means that you are never starting a generator from scratch. You can start with sample code created as part of the best practice, "Hand-Write Sample Code Before Generating the Code" and adjust the code from there. This will dramatically lower the startup costs for building a code generator.

Roslyn Is Immutable

Any operation performed on a Roslyn object will result in a new object. If you do not save and use this returned object, you will not see your changes incorporated and will get unexpected results. If you forget this simple fact, you can spend hours or even days wondering where your changes went. When using Roslyn, no other fact is more important to keep in mind.

Generating Code with Roslyn

Use Simple Objects to Host Metadata

Create a simple object to represent the metadata used to define the code being generated. This should include a read/write property from each table. This will help separate gathering and mapping the metadata from the code needed for the code generator. This separation can also allow you to potentially change the source of the metadata without having to change the code generator. Also, the code generator logic will be easier to follow if it does not have to deal with the more mundane details of retrieving and mapping the metadata.

Invert Business Logic

Inverting business logic will allow you to avoid nested conditionals. This will make the generated code easier to follow. Avoid nesting conditionals will also mean that more of the conditionals are also top-level conditionals, which are easier to generate. Any time we can simplify the generation process, we make it more likely that the code generator will be free from errors.

Consider the difference between the two methods shown in Listing 8-1.

Listing 8-1. Direct Interpretation Versus Inverted Logic

```
public string Rule1(IGreetingProfile data)
{
    if ((data.Hour <= 11) && (data.Gender == 1))
        return "Good Morning Mr. " + data.LastName;
    else return null;
}

public string Rule1(IGreetingProfile data)
{
    if (data.Hour > 11) return null;
    if (data.Gender != 1) return null;
    return "Good Morning Mr. " + data.LastName;
}
```

Reduce Complexity

Anything you can do to reduce the complexity of the code being generated will also reduce the complexity of the generator itself. Instead of checking to see if an input parameter's property has one of a handful of values, load the possible valid values into an array and see if the array contains the value from the input parameter. Adding values to an array of good values is much easier than adding an or statement to a conditional.

Reducing the complexity of the code generator will make it easier to write and debug, more likely to be free from bugs or defects, and allow you to get it written and tested more quickly.

Reflective Best Practices

Don't Lock the Assembly

For reflection to work, you need to load an assembly to load types from. Depending on how you load it, you may lock it so that it cannot be updated without first stopping your application. This is not always possible. The easiest way to load the assembly so that others can update it as needed is to read the contents of the assembly into memory and then load it from the byte array.

Reload the Assembly as Needed

Because we have made provisions for the assembly to be updated while the application is running, we also need to ensure that we are using the most current version of the assembly. Loading the assembly is too expensive to do every time its data is referenced. Instead, keep track of the modification date of the underlying file. If the modification date changes, reload the assembly. Otherwise, tell the program to continue using the assembly you currently have loaded.

Prefer GetTypes () to GetType ()

If you are interested in only one type, go ahead and call the GetType() method to get this type. But if you are interested in more than one type or potentially don't know which types you are interested in, GetTypes() is more efficient. The expensive reflection calls will be made only once. From there, you can apply whatever filtering you have to find the types you want.

There is one potentially dangerous caveat here. If *any* type fails to load, then no types will be returned from calling GetTypes(). The risk here is minimal because you have complete control over the generated assembly, but this can be problematic when you don't have such control.

Track Results

The point of using reflection is to systematically call every method in the types that you are interested in. This means that you need to track the results from these individual method calls. Usually each method will return a Boolean value, but your scenarios may differ. At any rate, you will need to track which method returned which result.

Keep the logic for calling each method separate from the logic for interpreting the results. Calling each method will be the same regardless of your specific scenario, but interpreting the results may be different every time.

Index

© Nick Harrison 2017
N. Harrison, *Code Generation with Roslyn*, DOI 10.1007/978-1-4842-2211-9

U

V, W, X, Y, Z

Get the eBook for only $4.99!

Why limit yourself?

Now you can take the weightless companion with you wherever you go and access your content on your PC, phone, tablet, or reader.

Since you've purchased this print book, we are happy to offer you the eBook for just $4.99.

Convenient and fully searchable, the PDF version enables you to easily find and copy code—or perform examples by quickly toggling between instructions and applications.

To learn more, go to http://www.apress.com/us/shop/companion or contact support@apress.com.